MW01259803

2022

Justa's Escape

Justa's Escape

A Journey from WWII Ukraine

Justina Neufeld
with Russell Binkley

Foreword by Beverley Olson Buller

RESOURCE *Publications* · Eugene, Oregon

JUSTA'S ESCAPE
A Journey from WWII Ukraine

Resource Publications
An Imprint of Wipf and Stock Publishers
199 W. 8th Ave., Suite 3
Eugene, OR 97401

www.wipfandstock.com

PAPERBACK ISBN: 978-1-6667-9526-4
HARDCOVER ISBN: 978-1-6667-9525-7
EBOOK ISBN: 978-1-6667-9524-0

05/11/22

Contents

Gerhard Sawatsky
11-25-1864 - 10-10-1925
Justina Wiebe
8-28-1864 - 1-5-1919

Peter P. Neufeld
9-19-1848 - 7-16-1922
Helene H. Peters
11-12-1851 - 5-10-1909

"Tante" Margaretha Wiebe
8-25-1874 - 3-30-1947

Anna Sawatsky Neufeld
9-21-1890 - 4-23-1965

Dietrich Peter Neufeld
11-1-1888 - 1941?

Dietrich & Anna Neufeld's family

Peter *Peta*
9-23-1911
- 1945?

Gerhard *Jeat*
3-8-1913
- 8-2-1985

Jacob *Jasch*
8-16-1915
- 12-24-2007

Dietrich
5-25-1918
- 10-7-1989

Johann *Hans*
1-14-1920
- 10-12-1998

Anna
10-18-1921
- 3-4-1999

Franz
4-25-1924
- 1945?

Willy
8-15-1926
- 2-17-2015

Bernhard *Bient*
8-1-1928
- 5-25-2006

Justina *Justa
Julie, Justel*
7-16-1930

Family Tree

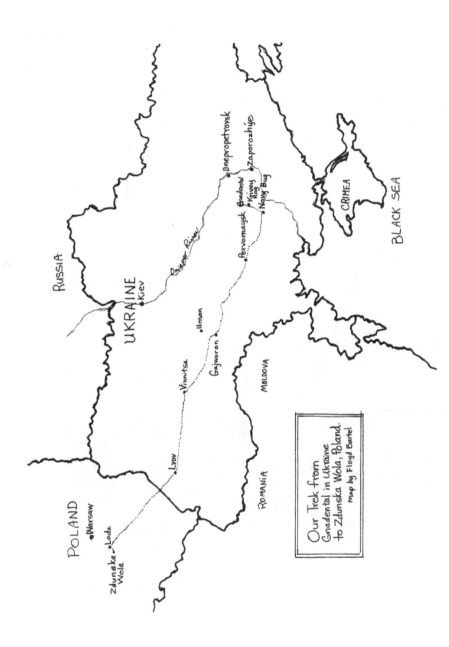

POLAND

Warsaw

Zdunska Wola • Lodz

RUSSIA

UKRAINE

Kiev

Dnieper River

Lvov

Vinnitsa

Uman

Gajworon

Pervomaysk

Gnadental

Krivoy Rog

Novy Bug

Dnepropetrovsk

Zaporozhye

MOLDOVA

ROMANIA

CRIMEA

BLACK SEA

Our Trek from
Gnadental in Ukraine
to Zdunska Wola, Poland.
map by Floyd Bartel

viii

Foreword

Books have long provided young readers with a way to vicariously experience pain, sadness, and hardship. The book you are holding does that for young readers today.

Justina Neufeld is a polished, friendly, knowledgeable professional with a past that informs her but is generally kept hidden. Now she shares in riveting detail the story of her hardships in and escape from war-torn Ukraine, the scattering of her family, her rescue by Peter and Elfrieda Dyck, and her eventual passage to the United States, where she has found a home. She recreates the world of her childhood, including tea parties with her best friend, counting butterflies, going barefoot from spring to nearly winter, and learning to swim in a cow pond. But she also takes the reader with her on the difficult travail across Europe as fighting approaches her small village in 1943 and the family must leave nearly everything behind. Sprinkled with words from and references to her Ukrainian culture, this book provides a visit to an earlier time and a long-gone world.

The journey Justina details in this book is not just one comprised of travel via rough wagons and troop ships but one of a young girl growing to womanhood, making important realizations about herself. At her lowest, Justina remembers thinking, "I could die before I grow up." Helping her mother recover from malaria prompts a desire that is later fulfilled: "I could be a nurse." Thankfully, reflection leads to the understanding that while there was pain and suffering, there was "much happiness later."

Young readers want to know "what happened next?" and do not like unfinished stories. Justina does not disappoint in that regard. She shares with readers her completion of high school, just a year later than her age group, her first date, and how she began sharing about her experiences at churches. Because she knows readers will wonder if her scattered family ever reunited, she includes a letter to the reader that fills in the blanks on her life until now.

Justina made friends wherever she lived. This same quality draws the reader in as she shares her incredible story of moving from a life filled with fear to a life of opportunity. I am proud to call her my friend and am thankful she decided to share her story with a younger audience.

Beverley Olson Buller
Author of *From Emporia* and *A Prairie Peter Pan*

I. My Name Is Justa

My name is Justina Neufeld,
but I have been called by other names.
One name was Justa, pronounced *Yoosta.*
They called me that at home.

I was born in Ukraine in 1930.
We had settled there because
in 1789, Russia's ruler,
Tsarina Catherine the Great,
invited my German ancestors to come
to farm Ukraine's fertile soil.
My village, called Gnadental,
was settled in 1872.
After the Russian Revolution of 1917,
they changed its name to Wodjanaja.

About fifty families lived in Wodjanaja
in buildings designed as an early leader had prescribed;
houses, all exactly alike—
even the number of rooms the same—
equidistant from the main street
and from our nearest neighbor.

I was the youngest of ten—
eight brothers, one sister.
Also living with us,
was grandmother's unmarried sister,
my great aunt (or *Tante*), Margaretha.

Justa's Escape

We called all grownups "aunt" or "uncle",
But I also thought of her as a grandmother
for mine had died before I was born.
The villagers called her *Tante Gretchen.*

For as long as I could remember,
five of my older brothers,
Peter, Gerhard, Jacob, Dietrich, and Johann,
were away in other towns and cities, studying.
My sister, Anna, brothers Franz, Willy, and Ben
still lived at home with my parents,
Tante, and me.

Bread was our staple.
We had no cereals.
We drank *prips*, a hot roasted barley drink
and ate bread for every breakfast—
but it was without butter or jam

One winter, there was no more flour to be had,
so Mama mixed spoiled corn flour, water, and salt
to bake *schnetje*, thick crackers
that were bitter and hard
because they had no fat or milk in them.

But, in summers we had enough to eat
because Mama grew food in our garden—
potatoes, carrots, cabbage, beets,
tomatoes, cucumbers, and watermelons.
She saved some in the cellar for winter,
and others she pickled in crocks.

When I was born,
communist Russia owned Ukraine.
Joseph Stalin was Russia's leader.
The Russian communists did not believe in God;

I. My Name Is Justa

"Religion is like opium—
It dulls people's minds,"
the communist philosopher Marx said
and Stalin enforced it.
He forbade religious gatherings.
He closed the churches,
and had some destroyed.
He seized Bibles and other religious books.
But some people—such as my parents—
believed in God anyway.
They taught us to pray,
to live as if God were watching.

My people were called *Mennonites*;
they believed only adults should be baptized,
that professing faith was a serious, grown-up decision,
and that Christians should not participate in war.
They had fled state church persecution,
moving from the lowlands of Holland to Germany.

Mama and Tante often sang hymns from memory:
We're marching to Zion, beautiful, beautiful Zion!
"Mama," I asked, "where is Zion?"
"It is far, far away," she replied.
"Not on this earth."
That puzzled me.
"Why do you want to go there?"
Mama smiled. "It will be better there.
We'll never know hunger there.
We will be safe.
We'll never be afraid."
Hearing Mama talk about safety made me realize
that she was also afraid.
Fear always hung over us.
I worried Papa would disappear in the night,
as so many other men and boys had.

Still, why would I want to leave my village
to march to Zion?
At least, not just yet.
But, I was a curious girl,
longing for adventure.
Perhaps, someday.
Then, I would set off to see—
this big world—
exciting places, interesting people.
I could never have predicted
the way I would see the world.

House Drawing[1]

1. Neufeld Family house drawing by Floyd Bartel. Courtesy of Justina Neufeld.

II. Playing

"You are a *rumdreeva*,"
(a gadabout), Mama scolded.
"Where have you been all afternoon?"
"Elsa and I played house—
first at Lena's, then at Elsa's.
We set tables with our *shoevels* (shards)
and invited guests to our pretend tea.
We had so much fun!"
I couldn't possibly relate all the other things
we had seen and done.
The whole village was our playground
and Elsa and I explored from one end to the other.
We knew everybody.
Everybody knew us.
We played so deeply,
that we were not aware time was passing,
so every day passed quickly.
"You have not gathered the eggs, yet.
Hurry! Supper is almost ready,"
Mama would say.

At mealtime, we all sat at our long table,
first folding our hands, then bowing our heads
for Papa's prayer.
Meals were for eating, not for talking.
Afterwards, Tante would wash the dishes.
I may go play, but I must not leave the yard.

II. Playing

At dusk, Tante closed the shutters
and lit the kerosene lamp.
If it was winter, we first did homework
and then we played games.
Ben asked Willy to play chess.
That left me out. I wailed,
"I want to play, too!
Let's play battleship instead."
The boys ignored me
So, I played with the cat.
Mietz was my pretend doll.
I dreaded bedtime.
When I said my prayers,
my chest felt squeezed.
by an invisible heaviness around me,
so it was hard to fall asleep.
Elsa's papa had disappeared at night,
and so had other men and boys
"Please keep Papa safe with us,"
I prayed over and over.

III. Letter from Ukraine

Mama told me about my cousin Lillian
who was close to my age.
Lillian lived in Canada with all Mama's brothers.
Mama got a faraway look and wet eyes
talking about her papa and her brothers
going away to Canada.
I could have been born in Canada—
I really wish I had—
but there were too many of us
to buy passports and pay fare.

When the letters from Canada stopped.
Mama said, "Our government
does not want us to know
how our people live in Canada.
Life is better for them.
They have enough food to eat all they want."
Here in school, teachers told my brothers,
Americans dumped wheat into the sea,
because they didn't want to share it.
They must have been very rich.
Lillian's papa had an automobile.
I had never even seen a real one—
only ones in pictures.

III. Letter from Ukraine

We weren't allowed to send letters to them, either.
"Go, Justa," said Mama,
"Write a pretend letter to Lillian."
So, I wrote a letter in my head.

Dear Cousin Lillian:
Next year I will be 8. I will start school. But I already know the alphabet. I can already read and write because my brothers Ben and Willy taught me. But numbers, I don't know so well, not like Papa. He used to figure numbers in some big flour mills before the Revolution.

Did you know Grandfather Sawatzky before he died? Papa says to tell my uncles to think of us. Please write me a long letter, Lillian. It would make Mama so happy.

Until we meet,
Your cousin,
Justa

IV. A Day I Will Never Forget; Abram has Died

My neighbor friend, Lena, was also eight years old.
One day, looking for adventure,
we sauntered though the village cemetery.
We saw flowers in full bloom.
Why not surprise our mothers with a bouquet?

At Lena's house, there sat her father on the porch.
Lena ran toward her papa.
"Look what we found!" she exclaimed,
holding out her fistful of blooms.

"And where did you two find these?" he asked.
"In the cemetery!" we answered, joyfully.
But Lena's father's face did not look pleased.
"You should never—no, never—take flowers *from* the cemetery!
You take flowers **to** the cemetery!" he said sternly.

My arms full of peonies sagged.
I lowered my eyes to the ground.
I had been so proud a moment ago,
but now I was full of shame.
I wanted our flowers to disappear.
I would not take them to Mama.
She, too, would not be pleased with my gift.

"Shall we take them back?" Lena whispered.
Her father shook his head.
"They will wilt there.

IV. A Day I Will Never Forget; Abram has Died

Put them in water and leave them here.
Look at them every day until they die,
so they will remind you of what you did.
Justa, you must come every day to see them. "
I handed Lena my bouquet.
I felt badly,
but I was relieved Mama would not know
what I had done.

Later, one summer morning, Lena,
breathlessly
entered our kitchen, nearly stepping on Mietz.
"Klassen's Abram is dead," she panted.
"Lena, are you sure?" Mama asked.
"Yes, it is true. I saw him!
His mama was crying real hard!
begging him,
Open your eyes,
but he would not."

Mama quickly removed her kitchen-stained apron
and tied on a clean one.
"And he just had the operation," she sighed.
She hurried to the Klassens next door
and Lena and I trailed her.
"You must not come in, now," she said firmly.
"I must help wash Abram
and get him ready for the funeral.
You can come later for that."

"A funeral?" I turned to Lena
Funerals are for when old people die!
Abram is the same age as Ben—
only two years older than us."
"How can he die already?' asked Lena.

Justa's Escape

We didn't feel much like playing.
Lena went home.
Much later, Mama returned.
"Now, Justa. You can go to see Abram."
Then Mama said,
"Take these irises and peonies for Tante Klassen."
I thought about the flowers we had taken from the graves.

I stopped for Lena and we hurried to see Abram.
The Klassens' front door was open.
A few neighbors had gathered and were talking quietly.
One woman motioned us closer.
"Go into the *koma*,
(the pantry, always the coolest room)
to see Abram."

Tante Klassen sat with folded hands,
next to the wooden box
that Abram's brothers must have made for him.
It balanced atop sawhorses
and Abram, wrapped in a white sheet,
lay in the box.
We could see his very white face.
He lay so still,
eyes closed.
Tante Klassen did not seem to notice anyone else.
Her lips moved, but we heard nothing.
It was an odd feeling for me.
How could a young person be dead?
I bowed my head,
folded my arms,
tiptoed silently from the *koma*.

Soon, a black-rimmed envelope was carried house to house.
It was the announcement of Abram's death,
with the date, time, and place for the funeral

IV. A Day I Will Never Forget; Abram has Died

which was to be the next day
in the Klassen's front yard.

The neighbors set up benches and chairs.
Abram's mother and four brothers sat
on one long bench
beside the ash-blackened box
that held Abram.
There was no papa in his family.
Years ago, he had been arrested
and disappeared.
The women wore black kerchiefs on their heads.
A neighbor woman read from the Bible.
We sang some sad songs.

After quite a while,
Abram's mother walked slowly
to kiss her dead boy.
She looked down at him for a long time,
and then pulled the sheet up over his face.
The brothers covered the box
with its wooden lid.
The men loaded the casket
on a wagon
and we all walked behind
the trudging horses
to the graveyard,
slowly.
Lena and I followed.
We had been to other funerals
and dreaded the sounds—
clods of dirt thumping on the box.
Such a day I will never forget.

V. I Want to Be Awake When They Come for Papa

If I pester Mama too long, she says,
"Go and pretend to write a letter to Lillian.
or to Uncle Ben.
Tell them about our family."
Whatever could I write to Uncle Ben?
But I can always write to Lillian.
Is she also writing to me in her head?
Mama says maybe our family sends us letters
but they get stopped at the border
because we aren't supposed to know
how things are better in Canada.
To me, life is not really so bad here
except when we are hungry
and can't buy flour for bread
or when I'm scared for Papa.

Wodjanaja, March 1938
Dear Lillian:

I have eight older brothers and a sister. Peter is 19 years older than I am. He studies in the city. Then comes Gerhard. He is away learning to be a teacher.

Jacob—we call him *Yasch*—is third oldest. Mama says he was her helper when I came along. Yasch was ready for grade five, but our school only had four grades so he would have had to walk five miles to another village. When school started, the older boys waited for Yasch. But he could not find his cap. He refused to go.

V. I Want to Be Awake When They Come for Papa

So he stayed home. Mama said, "if you stay home, you will help me with Baby Justa." (That was me). He was not happy. One time when I cried, Mama told me, Yasch rocked my cradle so hard he dumped me out on the floor. (He never liked noise!) The cradle landed on top of me and so I cried even louder.

Now, he comes home to visit in the summer and catches me singing (which I like to do). He says, "Tjeesche, tjeeschje", which means *quiet, quiet* in Russian. It embarrasses me when anyone hears me singing.

After Yasch, comes Dietrich, named for Papa. He is also studying to be a teacher. Johann, who we call *Hans*, is next. He studies French and English in Leningrad. Then there is my only sister, Anna, named after Mama. Then come the ones that are still at home: Franz, Willy, Ben, and me.

I left this letter unfinished
because Ben and Willy
wanted to play *battleship*
before bedtime.
They hardly ever let me play;
I did not want to miss it

Wodjanaja
one week later
Dear Lillian:

I am very sad and scared. Three nights ago, they took my best friend Elsa's papa away. I heard Papa tell Mama it was the secret police, the KGB. They came at night to arrest him. They also took some other men from the village.

Elsa cried at school the next day. She didn't wake up to see him being taken, but her mama saw them shove him into the black automobile and drive away.

Now, it is hard to fall asleep at night. I want to be awake when they come for Papa. I always say the prayers I was taught and I keep talking to God for a long time. "Dear God, "I say, "what would Mama and the rest of us do if they take Papa away?"

Your cousin,
Justa

VI. A Scary Night; Wodjanaja, 1937

It was a Monday.
I had gone to sleep, as always,
at the foot of Mama and Papa's bed.
I awoke in the middle of the night.
Something was not normal.
Through the open shutters,
a faint light entered the window.
I saw Papa and Mama
hurriedly dressing,
scurrying around.
I heard them frantically whispering.

"What are you doing?"
I asked, sleep in my voice.
"Shush!" Mama hissed,
her hand to my lips.
I was half asleep,
but still I felt the tremble in her hand.

Papa slipped his suspenders over his shoulders
and neared the window.
He opened it just a crack.
I listened.
I heard it with him—
a motor's distant hum.

Justa's Escape

"They're coming down our way," Papa murmured.
In that pale light,
Mama covered her face with her hands,
then fell to her knees at our bedside.
"Now they're at Peter and Helen's," Papa said.

Mama prayed, barely audible.
"God," she begged.
"Save us from the *Black Raven*."
The words chilled.
I knew something of what she meant—
the men we all feared—
secret police who prowled the streets
and took away men and boys,
who were never heard from again.

I crawled from bed,
and took Papa's cold hand.
He quivered, too.
Fear gripped me.
Papa must be sick.
"Papa, why do you shake?" I whimpered.
My tears began to flow
and Papa held me very tightly.
Keeping one eye toward the window,
he whispered in a rasp,
"My number may be up tonight.
Anna, I need you to get up
to bring me my bundle."

Papa quickly went to the kitchen
to find his shoes.
I followed.
He took his usual place
at the head of the table,
his head bowed.

VI. A Scary Night; Wodjanaja, 1937

Mama brought his bundle
that she kept stored in the wardrobe.
She placed a quickly cut piece of bread
and a cup of water before Papa,
but he did not seem to notice.

"Papa, where will you go?" I asked.
but he was silent.
"Papa, do you know these men?"
Still, silence.
I tried to cuddle up to Mama,
but she seemed to ignore me.
My tremors increased.
Here, even with Papa and Mama,
I felt all alone.
Time crept while we sat there waiting.
When we heard the motor turn over,
Papa rushed back to the bedroom window.
They are going north—" Papa said,
"now they are stopping at Yasch Ens's house."

Mama was crying in earnest now.
"Oh, no! Dear God!
Spare that poor family—
five children and a sickly mother!
They cannot survive without a father!"

Mama and Papa stood long by the window,
waiting for that awful sound to fade.
In the morning, news reached our house.
Six men—fathers, brothers, sons—
arrested and taken away.
But Papa was spared—
I thanked God—
but for how long?
Who were those other families thanking?

VII. July 16, 1938; Starting School

When I turned eight,
I was eager to start school.
I would have Mr. Martens for my teacher
and in my class would be my friends,
Elsa Enns and another Justina.

Our school was a brick building, painted white
with two large classrooms and one small one.
Would I be able to share a desk with Elsa or Justina?
Mr. Martens won't allow it, I thought.
He knew we were friends.
I worried that Sascha Peters would sit behind me—
he pulled his sister's braids—
and my braids were very long.
Some girls' hair was short,
but I was growing mine to be as long as Mama's—
so long, she could sit on it.

Our village had just one school.
It went from first grade to grade four.
Even though children started school at age eight,
I had already been learning at home.
When I was five,
Ben and Willy had begun teaching me reading and writing.
I remembered once they argued about what to teach me first.
They got louder and louder.
They woke up Papa from his nap
and from the next room

VII. *July 16, 1938; Starting School*

he told them to quiet down.
"Give me the slate!" I demanded.
I had had enough.
"I will do it myself!"
The three of us scuffled for the slate.
Papa flung the door open.
He swatted at Willy, at Ben.
But no punishment for me!
I felt guilty
because I had been as boisterous as my brothers.
But Papa was such a gentle man.
Do you know that was the one time—
the only time—
I ever heard him raise his voice?

The school was in the middle of our village,
about a quarter-mile walk.
We had to be there by eight o'clock
and we came home for an hour for lunch,
then back to school;
class finished at four in the afternoon.

First and second grades shared a room
as did third and fourth grades.
We brought our own supplies:
pencils, paper booklets, slates, and chalk.
The school furnished the textbooks.
Just as I'd hoped,
I shared a double desk with Justina Klassen!
At first, we competed for best student.
By second grade, she was number one,
and I had slipped a bit;
I cared more about socializing.

Since Ukraine was one of the 15
Soviet Socialist Republics,
our lessons were all in Russian,

which was difficult for me
because at home,
we spoke only *Plautdietsch*.
We also called it '*Low German*',
the language our ancestors spoke
in Friesland, northern Holland.
It was called 'low'
because the people who spoke it
lived in the lower part of the country.
The school rule was *Speak Russian Only*.
The teachers tried to enforce it.
But requiring Russian-only
on the playground was impossible.
We forgot about Russian at recess.

"When will you start to grow?"
the others taunted.
The teasing got to me,
but the gym bars provided the answer, I thought.
I hung upside down,
minute after minute,
my head throbbing
my legs aching,
exhausted.
"Justa, why do you do this?"
Here stood our teacher, Mr. Martens.
"She stretches herself to be tall like me!"
a nearby girl answered.
I felt my face redden.
Mr. Martens laughed.
"You are as tall as you should be.
Isn't it good enough for you
to be the fastest runner in the class?
Hanging from the bars
won't make any difference."

VIII. My Tante, the Storyteller

Tante told me a story:
A boy climbs a ladder by moonlight
to steal just one pear
from the neighbor's tree.
Stealing, he knows, is a sin,
but he wants the pear so badly
that he can already taste it.
He is at the ladder's top
just reaching for the perfect pear
when he looks up
at the brightly shining moon.
It seems the moon
is looking back at him.
He remembers
what he has been taught:
God sees everything at all times,
whether I am good,
or whether I am naughty.
"Is that a true story, Tante?"
I really don't expect an answer.

Tante's kerchief was in place,
tied neatly beneath her chin.
Her face was as round
as the moon in the story,
and wrinkled like the moon's surface.
Her nose was big.

Hazel eyes set far apart
twinkled to betray her happiness
or misted over when sad.
These eyes, I knew,
had seen much.
She had already lived so long,
even before I was born.

Tante,
Grandmother Sawatzky's sister,
never married.
When Grandmother died,
Tante moved in to keep house for Grandfather
and his five sons, my uncles.
After the Revolution,
Grandfather and his sons,
like many villagers,
feared the new Soviet government
would forbid their religion,
and so they moved to Canada.
Mama wanted to go, too,
but Papa did not have enough money
for passports and passage,
for seven children in all.

It was for Mama
that Tante, also, stayed behind.
She saw Mama's sadness
and that she needed her
with a houseful of children
and another coming soon.
Tante moved in,
already with us
when the last three,
Willy and Bernhard and I,
Justina, were born.

IX. It Is Cold in Our House

I shivered,
complaining, "I am cold!"
so Mama sent me to bed.
I burrowed into my *prosh*,
a box-like bed with four legs.
But I could not sleep.
My toes were swollen—
itchy, fiery red.
Papa heard me whimper
and so he knelt by my prosh.
"You have *chilblains*." he said.
Gently, he rubbed my feet.
"I will find real *schlorre* for you.
We need to keep your feet warm and dry."
The shoes we wore were not meant for winter.
Papa's comforting let me drift off to sleep,
dreaming of walking to school
through the deep snow
in real shoes.

X. Tante Remembers

Tante—
So much like a grandmother—
anchor, rock, angel—
always there,
always loving me,
always thinking the best of me.

When I could not sleep,
Tante was my regular storyteller.
As she sat by my *prosh,*
her hands stayed busy with darning and patching.
"Tante," I said,
"Tell me about when you were rich."
"My dear," she chuckled. "I was never rich."
"I worked for a wealthy family.
I lived with them on their large estate—
not in a village like this.
I took care of their children—
Henry and Lilly."
"But you," I interrupted,
"had white bread, butter, and jam every day!
As much as you wanted.
You were never hungry, you said.
That means you were rich."
"*Na, ja,* (well, yes)" Tante allowed,
"compared to what we have now,
I was rich."

X. Tante Remembers

I prodded her:
"Tell me again about Lilly's dresses,
about the ribbons she wore
in her curly blond hair—
about Christmas and the plates full of sweets—
about all the flavors
and what they tasted like."
Tante closed her eyes and smacked her lips.
"Sweet and sour," she whispered.
"My favorite tastes."
"Raspberry, strawberry, orange,
plum, cherry.
and marzipan.
I can smell and taste them now."
And then I slept.
Soon, again,
I would quietly slip to her secret place
where Tante hid the forbidden Bible
to sniff the fading scents
of those candy wrappers,
smooth, as if ironed,
tucked between the pages
so long ago.

XI. An Evening without Tante

Tante had gone to Bergens' house after supper,
but now it was late.
"Why is she not home, yet?"
I asked Mama.
"She'll be home soon," Mama said,
dismissively.
Still, I worried.
It was not like Tante to go out alone at night.
Another hour crawled by.
Bedtime.
Did she take her Bible?
I carefully lifted her mattress,
trying not to rustle the straw inside—
not to give my snooping away—.
nothing on the wire coils underneath.
I held my breath.
I lifted the gunnysack at the bed's head.
There lay the book in its black leather.
I slid my hand between its pages
where the candy wrappers were pressed—
aroma of strawberries,
faint lemon,
distant raspberries.
It was enough comfort for me.
I could go to bed to wait for Tante.

XII. Springtime in My Village

By our house was a narrow canal
that flowed east to west.
Usually, after winter,
the ice broke up quickly
and huge chunks
got stuck and piled up at the low bridge.
Then the water ran over both banks,
flooding our garden.

Now, the snow and ice had melted
and the canal moved once again.
It traveled quickly,
emptying into the watering hole
in the cow pasture outside the village.

Elsa and I were restless,
eager to be outdoors again—
ready to explore what spring had uncovered.
We searched for treasure,
to add to last year's collection:
"Look!" Elsa shouted.
"The other half of the plate
you found last year!"

I was just a bit jealous
that she found the first piece.
I waded deeper into the mud

and spotted a fleck of white.
It was a small teacup
with no handle.
I rinsed it,
revealed a red border—
poppies dotted the edge.
I ignored its chips and cracks
and thought it beautiful.
"This will go well," I judged,
"with my other *schoawels*."
Next time for tea,
I could set a long table.

With a few more finds,
we went off to seek
a private spot,
not too close to the pigpen
with its bothersome flies,
to hide our prizes.
We settled under the tall lilac bushes,
promising cool shade in summer.
But wait!
Here strolled Mama's quarrelsome hen.
She sat on her early nest of eggs;
I was not willing to argue with Speckle.
She was sharp-beaked and mean!
When last I reached under her
in the henhouse to gather eggs,
she fiercely pecked my hands,
and left bloody spots.

Finally, we decided
to compromise with Speckle;
we'll move closer to the fence—
it's almost as shady.
We could hardly wait

to invite friends to our pretend party.
Elsa's dinnerware set was larger
because every spring,
I forgot where I had hidden mine
from the year before
and I had to start collecting all over again.

But by late spring,
the canal was barely a trickle
and weeds choked the flow.
We tethered our goat
to reach the patches of green grass nearby.
I joined Tante as she milked Koz at noon.
I counted each kind of butterfly.
I spread out in the soft grass
and followed the gliding clouds.
What if I were Amelia Earhart? I thought.
I'd seen her in a newsreel
one Saturday
at the schoolhouse movie night.
I could be a pilot like her—
courageous and heroic—
unafraid to fly alone.

XIII. Other Signs of Spring

In our village, we measured time
by when birds returned.
In spring, the barn swallows came back.
Year after year,
as far back as I could remember,
they built a nest
under the boards
where the house and barn connect.
But last year,
sparrows stole their spot
and so the swallows
found a new place
beneath the eaves
by the front porch,
my own favorite spot
where I could watch.
And there they built
their new nest
in no time at all.
Soon, they laid eggs.
Tiny yellow beaks opened wide.
Parents flew in with long thin worms
to dangle over the babies' mouths.

"Mama," I called.
"the swallows are here—
that means I can go barefoot to school."
"Oh Justa, you had better not;

the ground is still cold.
You'd best wait until you hear the first *hoopoe*
before you take off your stockings and *schlorre*."
The hoopoe was my favorite,
pretty with its bright red crown,
pinkish body,
black and white wings and tail,
yet so hard to catch a glimpse of
as it kept to the high treetops.

But Mama made us wait
until she was satisfied
the ground was warm.
Then we could shed
the gray wool stockings
that she had knitted for us
in the long winter.
Then we went without *schlorre*
all the way until October,
or maybe even November.

At first, the ground tickled our tender feet,
but soon, even with scratches and cuts,
our feet toughened.

Spring was also the time
For *mest klunje*—
manure stomping..
We needed manure bricks
to fuel our ovens in winter.
We dug into the big pile
of pig and cow manure,
spreading it over our yard.
Then, we added a layer of straw.
All of us children,
neighbors, too,

Justa's Escape

saw this task as fun.
We trampled this mixture
with our bare feet,
hooting and hollering,
pounding and packing
into a smooth layer
eight inches deep.
Day-to-day,
we went from neighbor-to-neighbor,
lending our feet
to the village manure dance.

Then, steam rose from the manure
as it dried in the sun.
With a straight spade,
The grownups cut squares,
and set these on edge to dry.
When the manure bricks could be handled,
villagers stacked them in a beehive shape
to dry completely,
after which, we stored them
in sheds to be used as fuel in winter.

The stork and cuckoo
followed the hoopoe.
The same black and white stork couple
always flew back to their old nest
on neighbor Thiessens' barn roof.
I announced at school,
"The storks are here!"
and then we speculated
which classmate was likely
to get a brother or sister this year.
Every spring, I asked the old pair
to bring me a little sister.
I don't believe they ever listened.

XIV. My First Swimming Lesson

One warm day,
I almost learned to float.
Mary Janzen, my sister Anna's friend,
four years older than me,
was very beautiful.
I begged her
one too many times
to teach me to float.
"Yes, on Saturday
I'll take you swimming."
She added,
"you little pest!"

I counted the days.
"Three more days
and we'll be swimming.
I told Elsa.
"Mary will teach us to float."
Elsa laughed.
"In the cow's watering hole?
The water is freezing
and it's so muddy!
I saw the whole herd
wading around in it!"

I paid no attention;
"I have a new bib apron
just right for swimming.

Justa's Escape

Well, not new—
It was Anna's.
It covers all my front."
I wanted Elsa to care about floating
as much as I did.
"You will come, won't you?"
Elsa pondered,
"My apron is old.
It has a big hole in the middle.
And besides, the boys
swim with nothing on!"
"That won't matter"
I assured.
"There won't be any boys there."
Elsa still looked concerned.
"I'm growing up;
my *tette* are getting bigger."
I knew what she meant.
Even though I was still rather small.

Mary had whispered,
"you need breasts to float."
I knew I had none,
But I convinced Mary
I would be able.
I had a plan;
I would mound clumps of mud
on my chest;
they would help me float.
They did not.

XV. Bringing News; Moshe the Peddler

I sat close to our street fence
watching big ants busily foraging.
How would it be to live the life of an ant?
Would you know how small you are?
Would you feel you did not matter?
My concentration was broken—
other village children's clamor!

Over the bridge rolled a wagon,
pulled by a single horse,
hooves clopping on the wood.
"Mama! Mama! It's Moshe!" I cried.
As he had every summer,
the peddler arrived in the village.
Mama stopped weeding her flowers
and straightened up.
She shaded her eyes with her hand
and smiled.
"Indeed, it is.
Now we'll have news
from Kamenka."
(Papa was born in Kamenka;
four of his brothers still lived there.)
Moshe had grown up there, too.
He knew Papa and my uncles well.
Mama walked to the fence
to greet Moshe.

Moshe, barely five feet tall,
looked pitifully underfed.
He led Mishka, his weary horse,
who strained against the cart,
loaded full—
stacks of baskets and boxes.
Children followed the trudging pair;
"What do you have?"
they prodded.
But Moshe replied with questions.
all in Low German:
"What are your names?
How old are you?
Who are your parents?
Will your Mama come to see my treasures?"
But there was no need for the children
to fetch their mothers;
they already approached the wagon.

"*Prrr,* Mishka! (Whoa, Mishka!)
This is where we get to rest.
We are at Anna's house."

"Mama, will you buy me something?
Mama, I want a doll," I pleaded.
But Mama said nothing.
She greeted Moshe with a handshake.
"How good to see you, Anna!
I have news.
Your brother-in-law Herman
is very sick.
Unable to eat.
Instead, something is eating him."
Moshe noticed me tugging at Mama's apron.
He tapped my head, then lifted my chin.
"Justa! Little Justa! Your papa's little doll!

XV. Bringing News; Moshe the Peddler

Why do you stay so small?
Perhaps your Mama will buy the drops I have
that make you grow!"
Mama led Moshe to the house
for cold *prips* and *schnetje*.
"Oh, Anna," Moshe said, gratefully,
"How kind you are to this old *Kaufman*.
Will we see Dietrich at early supper?"

It was hard for me to be patient.
It seemed the two grownups could sit and talk
Yiddish on the porch steps forever.
Each uncle and aunt in Kamenka
was thoroughly discussed.
Moshe shared every little detail;
when would we get to the cart?

Still more children had gathered around
and, like me, they were impatient, too.
Finally, with a last sip of *prips*,
Moshe sighed, stood, and limped to his wagon.
First he tied a bucket of oats around Mishka's neck.
"I'll bring you a drink, soon," he promised.
Finally, he started to unload each basket and box—
one, two, three, and more.

"I have needles.
I have thread.
I have knitting needles for the *grossmama*.
There's drops and powders.
Treatments for sickness of all kinds.
I have ribbons, beads, and bangles for girls—
and buckles for boys."
He almost sang it.

Very, very carefully, but with great flare,
Moshe lifted the cover from a smaller box.
What a sight! I gasped. Combs!
Yes, combs.
Fine-tooth combs.
Lice combs.
Narrow-edged combs.
Broad-edged combs.
Gracefully curved decorative combs.
"White combs for light-haired girls
and dark combs for dark-haired girls."

"Please, Mama," I begged.
I wanted the comb
with the painted daisies.
But my persistence
could not move her.
Yes, I felt disappointed, but I already knew
that the world did not revolve just for me.
Still, I wanted to see what else Moshe had.
I pulled at this jacket.
"Hab jie uck Poppe jebrocht?" I asked timidly.
"Poppe? Poppe? Du welst eene Popp?
No! No, I have no dolls,
no dolls in my store."
Moshe tugged at my pigtails.
I could tell he felt badly.
"But there are beautiful combs
for Mama to buy for you."
He took out the curved one,
the one with painted daisies
and tucked it into my hair.

"Mama, please," I dared to beg,
"Can I have it?
But Mama shook her head,

lowered her voice.
In her hand,
she clutched a bunch of knitting needles.
"I have money only for these.
This winter you will learn knitting."

But, the shame of letting my friends
see my eyes water!
I quickly choked back the tears.
After supper, the other villagers gathered,
to see Moshe's treasures from far away—
mostly looking—
not many buying.
Not for a long time
had they seen such things
in the village store.
But, even so,
the bare essentials
were all they could afford.

That night, Moshe slept at our house.
I do not know where he lay down
because all our beds were taken.
Sleep came for me,
but I heard the murmur of Moshe and Papa talking
Yiddish and Russian and German—
sometimes a jolly chuckle
and later a low, serious tone—
far into the night.
They were friends.

In the morning,
Moshe left the village.
I got neither doll nor comb,
but yet I felt happy.
The peddler's little cart and horse

had brought excitement,
interrupted the everyday,
connected us to the world
when 15 miles was far away.
So much lay out of our reach—
people we loved,
things we wanted to have—
but someday, someplace,
I could have that comb
or even a doll.

XVI. The Gypsies

When Moshe had gone,
the next highlight of summer
was usually the coming of the gypsies.
It was when our wild pink roses bloomed
and apricots ripened in the sun.
When someone in the fields spotted
the caravan of wagons coming from the west,
workers hurried home to warn,
"The gypsies are here!"
Now, why were we children
both fearful and curious?
We'd heard whispers
that gypsies in the village
meant things went missing
from barns, houses, and gardens.
Sometimes children disappeared.
Just rumors, I know now
(because no one actually knew firsthand).

I must have been eight or nine.
I was at Elsa's, playing house
when we heard a neighbor shout,
"The gypsies are coming!
"They're at the crossroad!"
That was just two houses
from where we lived;
my heart raced as I ran home as fast as I could,

Justa's Escape

reaching our fence
as the caravan neared the bridge.
Mama stood watching at our gate.

"Slow down, child," she cautioned.
"You'll break your neck."
How could she be so calm
when such mystery and excitement approached?
Now, across our road,
the wagons clustered around the village well;
the gypsy horses drank.
Soon, the members of the train
scattered throughout our village.
A dark, beautiful woman walked up to us.
Her eyes, pitch black, as was her long hair—
gold hoops in her ears,
rows of bangles jangling on her arms,
her red shirt hung with glass beads,
a vibrant orange skirt with red fringe
hung just above her brown bare feet—
a fantastic painting come to life!

"*Zdrastwujtje, Babushka.*" (Hello, Granny)
Mama and the woman
spoke Russian for a while.
She reached for my mother's hand,
but Mama tucked it tightly
under her folded arms.
But not me!
I stuck out my hand boldly.
I wanted to know my future.

She traced the folds of my hand.
"Oy, yoy, yoy," she fussed,
with repeated headshaking.
"Hardship! Such hardship,

44

pain and suffering for the little girl."
Mama would have none of this
and she tried to pull my hand away,
but the beautiful woman would not let go.
"Yes, and much happiness later . . ."
She continued to speak,
but Mama drowned her out.
I wanted to know more,
of what the woman knew.

"Justa, you know we don't believe in this,"
Mama scolded.
Then, walking the woman
to our apricot tree,
they filled her deep pockets with fruit.
A flurry of movement distracted me.
"Mama, Mama! Look! our roses!"
Boys, some of the strangers,
pulled off the blossoms,
threw them at each other.
"Tell them, Justa," Mama said gently,
to pick them by the stems,
not just the petals."

I felt a chill, with both fear and wonder,
whenever I recalled
what the gypsy woman predicted for me.
Years later, I would wonder,
how had she known my future?
Someday, I would also look back on these wanderers—
they also had no country—
and how little kindnesses
could mean so much.

XVII. Mama Is Sick

Mama was sick.
She could not get out of bed.
The gypsy woman's fretful words,
"oy, yoy, yoy",
repeated over and over
in my head.
Last summer, Abram died.
Would Mama die, too?
Except for Tante and me,
everyone was gone during the day
A pain sat in my chest;
I kept busy so as to forget it,
but the sharp-edged lump remained.

I sent up my prayers:
"Please, please,
let Mama get better."
But she only got worse.
She lay in the dark,
her bedding wet with sweat.
She was helpless;
we held the cup for her to drink.
Each morning, Papa said,
"Stay home, Justa.
Make sure Mama drinks water."
I tried, but often she would
push the water away,

throw off the covers.
Her feverish words
made no sense.
Seeing her like this
scared me.
What will happen to Mama?
Papa came home at lunch
to see how Mama was.
He ate no lunch.
He hurried off to Sofieyevka
to fetch a doctor.
I heard Tante's whispered sigh:
"I hope it is not too late."
I had to be brave,
so I ran outside
to let out my tears

When Papa returned
it was almost dusk.
He was alone.
He had walked the ten-kilometer
round trip to Sofieyevka.
"The doctor could not come,"
Papa said.
"But he sent these pills.
He thinks it is malaria."
I was relieved.
If the sickness has a name,
I reasoned,
maybe Mama could be helped.
And I was right.
Within the week,
Mama began to recover.
Still weak,
she could now drink on her own.
Tante cooked.

I helped.
Someday, I thought,
I will be a nurse.
I will learn how to help the sick.
I will comfort children who are afraid
when their mamas suffer.

XVIII. Brother Hans Comes Home

Each summer, two brothers, at least,
came home from school.
One day was special
because my fifth-oldest brother Hans
surprised us with a visit.
Maybe he had sent us a letter,
but we had not received it, yet,
and our village had no telephones.
Even so, a few minutes into the visit,
the whole village had heard the news.
First, someone saw Hans on the road
from the Devladovo train station.
As dusk approached,
Peter Janzen sprinted up,
burst into the summer kitchen:
"Your Hans is almost here!"
After his arrival,
I went out to report to the other village children
who crowded the porch.
I proudly fielded their questions:
"What does he look like?"
"Does he wear *schlorre* or store shoes?
"Does he still wear glasses?"
"Does he speak Russian to you?"
"Where does he live?"
I felt very important,
the sister of someone famous,

who, unlike their brothers who stayed,
had left the village to study
in the big city.
And then Hans appeared,
filling the doorway.
"So, this is what I look like!" he teased.
"If you want to know more,
come back tomorrow.
I'm going to sleep now."

The next day, after supper,
Hans sat on the porch steps.
Elsa, Tina, and Peter were there.
Other neighborhood children joined us.
We all wanted to hear about life
In the big city of Leningrad.
"What do you do all the time?" asked Peter.
"I study languages—
French, English, German."
"Do you speak Russian?"
It was Elsa who wanted to know.
"Oh, I learned that in high school."
"Let me tell you what I do for fun—
I go to opera or ballet or sightsee.
I just came from Crimea."
It seemed none of us had ever heard
of ballet, opera, or sightseeing.
Hans described a ballerina,
her delicate costumes,
how she had to dance on tip toes.
Now, we girls wanted to be ballerinas.

Then:
"Do you know who Florence Nightingale was?"
We did not.
Hans taught us a history lesson.

XVIII. Brother Hans Comes Home

"In Crimea," he said, "in the 1850s,
there was a terrible war.
That's when Florence Nightingale showed up.
She was the first modern nurse.
If you leave this village,
you could do something great, too.
You could become a nurse
and save many lives.
Or maybe you could become a teacher—"
Hans looked at me—
"just like our brother Dietrich."

I did not like to hear about war,
the fighting and the wounding
and the dying.
But I wanted to hear about this woman,
someone who took charge
and saved many lives.
Florence Nightingale became my hero.
"I don't want to be a ballerina,"
I told Hans.
"I want to become a nurse."

Hans stayed home for only a short time.
When he had gone,
I missed his stories of faraway places,
but they showed up in my dreams.
Elsa remembered Hans
and the message he brought,
"Maybe Hans was right," she said.
"When we grow up, we can leave this village."
I thought of how I would soon be nine.
"Maybe when I'm 20," I replied.
"I will go to see the world."

XIX. Summer Chore

What I dreaded most
was gathering eggs from the henhouse.
By the end of summer,
we had 30 to 50 chickens.
Then, in fall and into winter,
they were butchered for Sunday dinner.
By spring, only a few were left.

In the summertime,
chickens would fend for themselves.
They had the run of the whole yard.
They scratched for worms
around the pigpen
or on the huge manure pile
behind the barn.

When school was out,
my chore was to
collect the eggs
in the chicken house.
I would raid the nests
high up along one wall—
I had to climb up on a stool to reach.
In spring, the hens began to leave
their new-laid eggs
to search the yard for
a stray kernel of grain

or the odd weed.
Soon, some got the urge
for brooding,
to hatch their chicks.
They sat on their nests
as I tried to coax them off.
Stubborn, they ruffled their feathers,
made themselves look twice as big.
They loudly clucked a warning,
scolding me as I dared,
my reluctant hand beneath them
retrieving the warm smooth egg.
Sometimes, met by ferocious pecking,
my hand bloody,
I ran crying to Mama,
"Look what *Kookla* did to me!'
"It will heal, "Mama said,
matter-of-factly.
Back then, we had no *Band-Aids.*
Mama merely wiped the blood
with her apron's corner
and sent me back to the henhouse.

Mama thought she knew
when and where the hens would brood.
She chose a promising hen,
set up a cozy nest with fresh straw and eggs
and waited.
But another hen or two might play tricks;
They'd lay their eggs in an out-of-the way spot—
maybe hidden under the lilac bush
or behind the barn in a pile of straw.
Then one day,
here hen and babies would come,
marching all in a line,
in front of Mama

as if the hen were showing off.
"Well, well! Where did you come from?"
Mama would ask.
"You fooled me again!"
But she was happy to see them.

XX. Butchering Day

It was at the first frost,
a month after school had begun—
butchering season in the village.
It felt festive to all of us!
Excitement!
Anticipating eating well.

Days ahead, we were preparing:
sharpening knives,
scouring pots,
baking bread,
filling big pans with zwiebach,
the bun with a top.
On that day,
the fattest hens or roosters
were chosen,
sacrificed for our noon meal.
We plucked their feathers
and over the fire,
singed off their down—
a sickening smell.
Before dawn,
neighbors, two couples,
came to help.
Mama set out breakfast:
prips, fresh bread,
a pan of new cracklings,

a recent gift from a neighbor's
own butchering day.
Each year, I begged to stay home
from school,
but only succeeded once,
for Mama believed me
when I claimed to be sick.

Waking, I covered my head with my pillow,
to keep from hearing
that poor pig's final squeal.
On a rack over a trough,
they lay the slaughtered hog.
The men drenched it with scalding water,
so they could scrape off the bristles
with their sharp blades.

Brother Ben had claimed the tail,
attached it to a large safety pin,
and tucked it into his pocket.
He planned to get back at Yasch Klassen,
so he was eager to get to school.
Last year, Yasch had brought a pig's tail
and sneakily pinned it to the seat of Ben's pants
without his knowing it,
and when the teacher called Ben
to the blackboard to work a math problem,
the class erupted in giggles.
The teacher had to bite his lip
to keep from laughing.
This year, it would be Yasch's turn
to wear the tail.

The pig was in parts by lunchtime.
I waited my turn,
because the helpers ate first.

XX. Butchering Day

The wonderful smells from the kitchen
were almost too much to bear.
It was crisp and juicy chicken,
with a fruit dressing on the side called *bubbat*.
There were dishes of dill and watermelon pickles—
part of the feast like no other.

Back at school, I thought about
the action I was missing at home.
They were cooking spareribs,
and liverwurst
in the big lard rendering cauldron.
The tongue, the heart, the feet—
even the ears—
they'd mix with seasonings
and put into a covered crock—
becoming another tasty meal
in a few days.

Each neighbor-helper was rewarded:
a ring of liver sausage, some spareribs.
The next day would be another butchering
at another house,
neighbor helping neighbor.

XXI. Waiting for Papa

My country's communist government
would not let us practice our religion.
So, instead of celebrating Christmas,
we observed New Year's Day
when Father Frost
brought presents for us.
Father Frost wore
a long snowy fur coat
and fur hat.
Children loved him.
He was like a jolly grandpa.

But we had to keep a secret.
Our parents whispered
that the real holiday
came a week before.
That holiday was Christmas.
We heard about the special baby
born many years ago.
So, we pretended to
welcome the New Year,
but it was really Christmas
we were marking.

On New Year's Eve,
our parents showed us—
as when they were young

XXI. Waiting for Papa

we could set out a plate for St. Nicholas,
hoping in the morning
we'd discover he'd left sweets for us.

It was late December.
I must have been nine or ten.
Papa had to make a business trip
to buy supplies for the collective farm.
Because it was very cold,
he pulled on his felt boots
and wrapped up in the sheepskin-lined
long family overcoat.
"Papa, when will you be back?"
He could not miss
my part in the school's program
on New Year's Eve!
Papa tugged my pigtails.
"I'll be home the day before.
You'll see me in the front row!"
"And, Papa," I added,
"Please bring us some *halva*
and *rakoveye schaky* (hard candy)
to have a real Christmas
like you used to have!"
Papa smiled and winked,
"If the store has it,
I'll bring you some."
Papa would have to hitch a ride
the ten kilometers
to the railway station.
to board the train to Dnepropetrovsk.
Mama shook her head
as she watched him trudge away.
"I wish he wouldn't go,"
she fretted to Tante.
"The weather can change any time.

Justa's Escape

The winter storms from the east
have missed us so far, but . . . ,"
she did not finish.

I woke up.
It was Friday,
the day before our New Year's program.
The ground was blanketed
in deep powdery snow.
I walked in Ben and Will's footsteps
all the way to school.
It could be hard
in snow or mud
to keep the *schlorre*
with their wooden soles
and leather straps
on my feet.
A new wave of heavy snow
blew in and drifted before noon
so school was called off.
We started for home.
I lost one *schlorr.*
The wind blew snow into my eyes;
Blindly, I searched the snow,
but I could not find the missing *schlorr*
and I called to my brothers,
but the storm stole my voice.
About to panic, my tears froze
A sudden hand gripped my arm.

It was my teacher.
"You must hurry home!"
He held me firmly
until Ben struggled back to help,
but the missing *schlorr* was not to be found.
Cold and wet, home at last,

XXI. Waiting for Papa

Mama mildly scolded me.
"We'll not find it
until the snow melts."

Bitter air followed.
Mounds of snow piled up,
blocked the door.
After supper, the oven fire died.
Chill settled into the house.
Thick frost built up inside the windows.
It was so different from other evenings.
Usually, Mama and Tante sang together
as they knitted, sewed, or patched.
Now, Mama's mood was cross
and Tante washed the dishes silently.
Even my boisterous brothers stayed quiet.
I practiced my lines for the program,
then half-heartedly played with Mietz,
but could only think of Papa
and the blizzard outside.

"When will Papa come home?"
I asked yet again,
and Mama could only say,
"He said he'd be home before New Year's Eve."
Mama had told Ben to make a peephole
by breathing on the windowpane
for the lamplight to shine through.
When we heard an urgent knock at the door
I was sure it was Papa coming home.

But it was a neighbor, Onkel Thieszen
carrying a note from house-to-house,
announcing the New Year's Eve program
would not take place because of the weather.
"Did you know," he asked, gravely,

Justa's Escape

There are wolves howling near the livestock barn?
Don't go out into this blizzard!"
We reminded Ben to keep the peephole open
so Papa would see the light.
Every so often, he blew on the glass
and scratched with his nails to clear
the thick ice from the windowpane.
Now, the drifts reached
the lower halves of our windows.
Though wrapped in blankets,
we shivered.
Hands blue with cold,
Mama kept knitting.

At bedtime, we set out plates
for Father Frost.
I was hoping for a doll,
some halva and candy.
I'd never had a real doll
so I'd pretend with Mietz.
That night, I prayed
several times over
so God would be sure to listen
to my pleading for Papa's safe return.
I was not supposed to hear
Ben and Willy tell stories
about packs of wolves
attacking people in sleighs.
"If Papa has to walk home,
the wolves might get him."
Willy whispered.
I could not fall asleep
with such thoughts in my mind.

I crept to the kitchen
to wait with Mama.

XXI. Waiting for Papa

She stood by the window,
breathing on the peephole,
peering into the darkness.
She brought her apron corners
to her face.
Was she wiping her tears?
My heart pounded.
I shivered in the doorway,
though wrapped in my blanket.
I stammered out my fears.
"Can wolves eat grown men?
Will the snow cover our house
as Ben said?"
I was fighting back tears.
"You go back to bed," Mama said.
"I will do the waiting for all of us.
"Papa said he would be back by New Year's Eve."

Was I trembling from fear or from cold?
I snuggled into Papa's place in bed.
Folding my hands,
I prayed again.
"Dear God. I don't want any presents.
No sweets. No doll.
Just bring Papa home.
Amen."

Before I knew it, I had awoken myself with a shriek.
Something icy had touched me.
The room was dark as pitch.
"Justa," whispered a familiar voice
"It's your papa."
I untangled my blanket
and flung my arms around his neck.
Papa was safe at home!
Feeling such relief, I fell asleep

in my place at the foot
of my parents' bed.

I got up first, in the dark early morning.
I ran to the kitchen table.
Father Frost's plates were empty!
Instead, I found a package in oily newspaper.
As I peeked at the parcel,
it almost unwrapped itself,
revealing a chunk of dark coarse *halva*!
"Papa, you remembered," I whispered.
"I'm waiting for Papa to get up,"
I whispered to Mama as I stood by the bed.
"Shh, child," Mama hushed.
"He just got to sleep
and I don't think he can get up today.
I think his toes were frozen.
Come back to bed while I go start the fire."

But Papa stirred, "I am not asleep."
I nearly jumped into bed.
"Papa, did you see the wolves?"
"No, Justa, I did not.
All I could hear was the howling wind."
"But why were you so late, Papa?"
"I was lost in the storm," he said.
"All of yesterday and last night."
"But, Papa, I knew you'd keep your promise
to come home for the New Year!"

At breakfast, Mama blew over
the hot *prips* in her saucer,
with eyes fixed on the icy windowpanes.
"After the wind let up,"
she said to Tante.
"Dietrich was exhausted,

but he would not let himself stop walking.
He scooped up snow to quench his thirst
and ate bits of *halva* to give him strength."
"It's good," Tante sighed,
"that he didn't stop.
It saved his life."
If Willy hadn't shoveled
the snow away from the windows,
he wouldn't have seen our light.
After a long sip of her hot drink,
Mama continued.
"I was dozing off from knitting
when I heard scritching
at the window.
I could scarcely force the door open.
I saw this dark heap before the window.
'Is that you Dietrich?' I called,
and no one answered.
But the heap crept towards me
and I hardly recognized him
as I pulled him inside."

We spent a quiet day so Papa could sleep.
He woke up late in the afternoon
when the outside was bright with reflected light.
Mama soaked his feet in warm water
and then rewrapped them.
"Do they hurt, Papa?" I asked.
"Yes, but not so much as before.

XXII. 1941; My World Turns Upside Down

Life should have been carefree.
School was out for summer,
but these were somber days.

I was almost eleven years old
when the village news loudspeaker announced
"Germany is at war with us."
The news had come
over the village's only radio
in the government office.
Mama wrung her hands,
wiping tears with her apron.
"Where are my boys?" she asked,
as if searching for them
in the distance.
"If only I'd insisted
they'd come home for the summer."
"Now, Anna," Tante softly reminded,
"you know there is no work
for them here
to earn money for school."
"Is the war coming here?"
I had to ask.
But Mama seemed not to hear.
Distractedly, she left the kitchen,
to sit under the pear tree
in the garden
where I knew she felt free to cry.

XXII. 1941; My World Turns Upside Down

At supper, dread hung over the table.
Papa and Mama talked quietly
about my brothers.
Would they be made to fight
in the war?
Such uncertainty frightened me,
but I wanted to hear.

Mama sent me away
to help Tante with the dishes.
With trembling and slippery hands,
I dropped a plate;
It shattered.
"Go, Justa. Go out and play,"
Tante urged.
How could I play?
Even though Mietze purred for my attention,
I had no interest in her.
I tried to eavesdrop,
but the grownup's voices were just murmurs.

When I was sent to bed,
all I could think about was the war.
Sleep came at last,
but I awoke to the sound of Mama's sobs.
The bed was empty.
Mama knelt in the darkened room;
she was praying.

Early one morning,
Mama shook me awake.
Papa was working nightshift.
"Justa," she said,
"I need you to go get Papa from work.
His breakfast is ready."
Had she been crying?

Justa's Escape

Uneasily, I obeyed,
though wishing she would go herself.
I walked behind the houses
to the collective farm's dairy barn
where Papa had his office.
I entered the barn with its rows
of tied–up munching cows
waiting to be milked.
Tante Peters looked up from her milking stool.
"What are you doing here?"
She sounded unfriendly,
but why?
"I came for Papa—for breakfast,"
I stammered.

Something felt wrong.
My chest tightened;
my breath became short.
"Your papa?" Tante Peters replied.
"Go tell your Mama they took him away last night—
the NKVD—
the secret police. "
With that, I ran from the barn.
I tried to shout, to scream,
but no sound came out.
This message
lay like lead inside of me—
too much for a little girl.
How could I tell Mama such news?

A mistake.
Yes, it must be a mistake!
If I prayed hard enough—
I could make it not so.
A miracle would happen
and Papa would come home.

XXIII. A Letter to Lillian

30 August 1941
Dear Lillian,

We still cannot send letters, so I am writing to you again in my head.

This morning, when I woke up, a German soldier was eating his breakfast on our porch. Mama let him sleep in our parlor last night. He brought his breakfast back to our house from the army kitchen. I could not help watching him with my hungry eyes. "Justa," Mama scolded, "Come here. It is not polite to stare at a guest's plate while he eats." "But, Mama," I said, "He has white bread and butter! He must be very rich!"

The soldier stood up and walked into our kitchen. He said, "*Kleines Maedchen, hier, nimm ein Stueck Butterbrot.*" He offered me a slice of his buttered bread. I was eager, but also embarrassed, I could feel my face burn. I had not known he could understand when I talked about his bread in Plautdietsch. Still, I was quick to gobble it up before my brothers came in to claim it.

Later that day, I was surprised to hear Mama and Tante in the kitchen, singing once again.

"*Lasst die Herzen immer froelich
und mit Dank erfuelet sein . . .*"

(Let your hearts be ever joyful and filled with thanksgiving . . .)

They have not sung since Papa was gone. What did this mean? Were they singing because of what Dietrich said about the prisoners being released was coming true? I will write more when Papa comes home.

Your cousin,
Justa

XXIV. Church

It's been two weeks
since the Germans captured Dnepropetrovsk.
Yet, Papa has not come home.
We wait and wait.
Each night I lie awake,
sometimes very late,
listening for the door to open,
but I fall asleep and when morning comes,
there is no miracle;
he is still not here.
Can you understand the empty place
in a heart when the papa you love is gone?

Each evening,
we see bright light on the eastern horizon.
Dietrich says the Russian
army is running away,
retreating, he calls it,
burning the grain fields and buildings
so that when the Germans get there,
nothing will be left but rubble.
Such destruction is hard for me to picture.
Our village has finished with the harvest.
Before, farmers had to deliver
all their crops to the government,
but because of the war,
no one is here to take it.

XXIV. Church

For the first time in a long while,
we have enough milk;
we have enough butter.
The villagers have re-divided the land
and again will farm for themselves
instead of for the government.

Some people think the communist government
is gone for good.
Now, Mama and Tante are so glad
they can have *Andacht* (church) again.
They told us how much they missed it,
so I wanted to see why.
But, when Sunday came,
Mama said it was only for grownups.
Children could not understand the preacher.
Eventually I'd be welcome
in special classes just for children.
But, I begged and begged,
and I wore her down.
So excited, I ran ahead
as we walked to my school.
Andacht would be in a classroom.
I was the only child in the room!
First, an old man read from the Bible.
I knew this book had been forbidden
after the big revolution
because Tante kept hers so well-hidden.
Then, they sang songs, which I knew,
because Mama and Tante sang them at home
all the time.
All at once, everyone fell to their knees
and prayed aloud all together
Many sobbed,
praying for fathers and brothers
whom they had not heard from

since they had been arrested.
It made me afraid—
this loud crying and pleading.
I was ready to go home,
never to come again!

XXV. New Teacher, New Language

Since the German occupation,
we could safely speak German again.
Even the village went back
to its German name, *Gnadental*
At home, we still spoke *Plautdietsch*
but school was now all in German.
Although the language was familiar,
(in Mama's and Tante's songs)
I had never spoken, read, or written it,
but now I was learning it.
In school, the foreign language we learned
was Ukrainian—
which was funny to me—
we lived in Ukraine!
And in fourth grade,
I had a new teacher, Mr. Neudorf.
No longer did we write the Russian Cyrillic.
Would I forget to speak and write
the beautiful Russian?
Never!
Dascha and Anya,
my two Ukrainian sisters-in law,
still spoke Russian to me.
We sang German folk songs,
peppy and fun
"Alle Voegel sind nun da, alle alle alle . . . . . ."
and *"Mein Hut, er hat drei Eken,*

drei Eken hat mein Hut". . . . . . .
I was getting used to the new language,
but not to Mr. Neudorf.
He was strict,
always watching us closely.
Every time we whispered or giggled,
he caught my seatmate,
Julia, and me.

XXVI. 1943; The War Goes On

Although Papa was gone for two years,
we still waited for him.
I was storing up things to tell him.
In his absence,
big brother Dietrich helped Mama make decisions.
"The German Army is retreating;
we have to be ready to leave ahead of them,"
he told Mama.
"Because we are Germans,
the Russian Communists will not treat us well."
Mama's voice shook.
"Where will we go?
When Papa comes home,
he will not know where to find us!"
Leave without Papa? I thought.
My stomach heaved.
How can Dietrich even think of that?
I will never leave without Papa!
Never!

XXVII. October 22, 1943; The Front Approaches

"The fighting is getting closer," said Dietrich.
And, of course, we know he is right.
We heard explosions
day and night.
"We'll be in the line of fire soon."
I shivered when I heard him say that.

We began to accept
that we must be ready to leave our home,
our beautiful dear village,
our winter food supply,
two fat hogs,
our chickens, and geese.

Our horses,
Kunta, Sashka, and Gorka
had been shoed.
Mama had Franz cover the ladder wagon
with a tarp
over its wooden frame.
Dietrich and Dascha had already left
with their little Hilda.
Now, at eighteen,
Franz was the oldest boy at home.

The morning we left was tense.

XXVII. *October 22, 1943; The Front Approaches*

I woke up early;
Franz was already impatient with Willy and Ben.
"Don't you know anything
about loading a wagon?
Bundles of bedding go in front
where Mama and Tante will sit!"
he snapped.
The food goes next,
then the sewing machine
and then the clock.
And in the back,
the oats for the horses."

The explosions seemed closer than ever,
and so I was fully awake.
Yesterday,
the hubbub of getting ready
filled me with excitement
to be going on this journey.
I thought of seeing big cities
and meeting new people.
Now, that feeling was gone,
replaced with emptiness,
an almost painful gnawing
in the pit of my stomach.
It was real.
We were leaving without Papa.

When the loading was finished,
Franz helped Mama and Tante
climb into the wagon.
I picked up Mietz, and followed Tante.
"Not you," Franz said firmly,
"You will walk with the rest.
And, leave that cat here!"
Abandon Mietz?

Justa's Escape

My eyes overflowed.
I would not—could not—leave her behind.
I clutched my dear Mietz tightly
as I fell in-step beside my sister, Anna.
Our wagon pulled onto the road,
joining a line of others,
from north and south and east,
as far as I could see
on the road to the west.
I tried to spy Elsa's family—
Maybe we could walk together.
Maybe it was fright,
or maybe it was just
not wanting to leave her home,
but Mietz started suddenly,
clawing,
wriggling from my arms,
and she was gone.
"No." Anna said, firmly
as I tried to follow.
"Let her go.
This is where she belongs.
We don't know where we will end up."
At last, a flood of tears came.
I hid my face so Franz would not see –
would not call me a crybaby.

I walked ahead to look for Elsa.
The talking and clatter
of the horses and people and wagons
must have muffled
the hum of the distant aircraft
until it was too late.
Suddenly, we were strafed.
Bullets hummed by me
as I dashed back to the wagon.

XXVII. October 22, 1943; The Front Approaches

Mama and Tante climbed down.
The leader shouted,
"Into the ditches, everyone!"
Mama grasped her side,
her face contorted in pain.
Had she been struck?
We scrambled face down
in the ditch.
The strafing went on.
I begged God for protection.
"Let us live, please."
My heart galloped madly,
breath quickened by terror.
Then silence.
The airplanes were gone.
The caravan began to return to life.
We crawled up to the road.
Mama could tell what I was thinking.
"It's just my old sciatic trouble, "she says,
rubbing her hip.
The horses had been spooked into the fields,
dragging the wagons in all directions.
It took time to untangle their gear
and match the travelers
with their belongings.
Once again, the caravan resumed its trek.
The leader directed us:
"Drive, drive! Drive as fast as you can—
the fighting is close behind!
Thank God," he added,
"no human life was lost."
Later we learned,
some of our sheep had been killed
and the village herd was scattered.
We left them behind
in our desperate rush

to get ahead of the conflict.
So, Franz snapped the reins
and the horses took off.
With no livestock to tend,
Willy and Ben joined Anna and me
as we strode beside the wagon.
We crested the last hill
from which you could see the village
nestled in its valley.
Mama looked back one last time,
tears glistening on her cheeks.

Late afternoon.
Mama handed us a slice of bread
and a piece of fried chicken.
We ate as we walked.
My *schlorre* rubbed a blister
on my little toe.
I stepped out of them
and walked barefoot
in the soft dust.
Tired. Hungry. Sad. Dirty.
We had traveled 35 kilometers
in our village caravan of 30 wagons
and dusk was gathering
when we reached *Krivoj Rog*.
The roads were clogged with other refugees
and military equipment.
Franz sent Ben to find water for the horses.
Anna took a pail with her
to bring back water for us.
I had looked for Elsa all day
and finally spotted her family's two gray horses.
She, too, had gone to look for water.
Elsa's family expected more from her.
It struck me how lucky I was at 13,

XXVII. October 22, 1943; The Front Approaches

to be the youngest,
to have an older sister
and older brothers
who took on all the chores.
With only one older brother
and two younger ones,
Elsa, the oldest girl in her family had more chores than I had.
When I headed back to the wagon,
I felt a growing panic.
But where had it gone?
Had they left without me?
Night had come—
irritable voices of families,
bleating, distressed farm animals,
roaring of army truck motors.
I ran to and fro.
No wagon!
I was lost
in a crowd of milling strangers.
Finally, I stopped,
frozen.
They are gone!
I will never find them.
From behind,
A rough hand clutched my arm.
My heart stopped mid-gallop.
"Don't you ever wander off again!"
Franz thundered.
Meekly, I followed him back to our wagon
where Mama had begun
to hand out pieces of chicken and bread.
From now on, I pledged to myself.
I would love and obey my brother,

Krivoj Rog's lights were dim

so, the intermittent explosions
lit up the sky brilliantly.
Mama passed out our bedding.
We were to share pillows and blankets.
We bedded down under the wagon
just as the sky flashed as bright as day.
"Look!" Uncle Peters marveled,
both armies are fighting over the city!
We're seeing crossfire."
A huge ball of fire blazed on the horizon
followed by a horrific boom
that sounded very close.
Mama reacted by throwing her pillow over me.
The ground under us trembled.

Once again,
I realized I could die before I grew up,
before I'd visited big cities,
attended a real ballet,
studied to be a nurse,
or became the mother
of my six imaginary children.
Now, explosion followed explosion
with scarce time between.
"The city is on fire!"
I heard a young voice cry.
"Mama, we have to go!"
another young voice urged.
"Children, come close,"
their Mama answered.
"We have nowhere else to go.
All we can do is pray."
She was resigned.

1. Mennonite Library and Archives Photo Collection, 2005–012. Copyright © Bethel College. Used with permission. https://mla.bethelks.edu/archives/numbered-photos/pholist2.php?num=2005–012

XXVIII. The Journey Continues

Mama nudged me.
"Justa, get up quickly;
we are ready to leave."
Daylight was just creeping in
and I was still tired.
Mama handed me a hot enamel cup
and a slice of bread.
She whispered something to Franz,
who answered grouchily,
"Well, if there is room in the wagon,
I guess she can ride for a few hours."
Mama helped me up on to the wagon
where I squeezed in next to Tante.
Soon, despite the jostling
and the rattles,
I was again asleep.

When I woke,
We were on the road's shoulder,
plodding along beside
a stream of military vehicles.
A German soldier on horseback
sauntered along beside us.
As he rode,
he ate from his mess canteen
He looked directly at me
and gestured and nodded at his container,
"You want some?" he asked.

XXVIII. The Journey Continues

A bit fearful, I shook my head *no*,
but Willy saw and intervened.
"Yes, yes, she does!"
he answered for me.
The soldier promptly handed me his kit.
Oh, such delicious stew, I thought,
tempted to devour it
in just a gulp.
But I restrained myself
and shared some with Willy.
We wolfed it down
furtively,
so we'd have it all.
Boldly, Willy said "ˆ*bolshoe* spaseebo*,"
as he handed back the empty container.
The soldier smiled broadly,
his teeth very white
beneath his thick black mustache.
Willy said, "He is Romanian;
they have joined to fight the communists."

After a long day,
the wagons left the road.
We unhitched the horses
by a haystack in a field.
Ben and Willy went off
to search for water.
The horses needed to drink
and Mama had stew in mind.
It was Anna's and my job
to find kindling and firewood.

Mama reached in the gunnysack—
carrots, onions, potatoes—
and from the crock,
a chunk of meat.
Franz set up the iron tripod

on which the kettle would hang.
He lit the twigs.
"Now, where are those boys
with the water?"
He was impatient.
"We can't cook after dark!"
I asked why
and he gave me a look
as if I were stupid.
"They could see the fire
from the air
and bomb our camp.
That's why!" Franz retorted.

All around us,
little fires had appeared
as each family cooked supper.
But when darkness came,
not a single flame remained.

Someone was strumming a guitar
and soon there was singing;
> *"Take Thou my hand, O Father, and lead Thou me*
> *until my journey endeth eternally . . . ."*

In the middle of nowhere,
surrounded by darkness and war,
we sang a few songs of thanksgiving,
and then the silence gathered.

Some bedded under their wagons,
but Mama and I nestled in the hay.
"Don't forget to pray, Justa,"
Mama reminded me,
but sleep overtook me
before I finished.

XXVIII. The Journey Continues

A gray day began,
cold and rainy.
The wet wood would take no spark
so we had no hot drink to warm us.
The road was muddy and deeply rutted
which made driving the wagons treacherous.
The muck strained the horses;
travelers tried to lighten their loads,
abandoning their belongings—
a chair, a chest, a bundle—
in the surrounding fields.
Monotonous—
on the move by day,
marked by explosions—
sometimes near,
sometimes distant.
Where is the warfront today?
we wondered.
How close is the fighting?
I was ready to turn back,
to go home.
I had longed for adventure—
some excitement to color my everyday life—
but this was not like I had imagined.

Soon, our food supply had dwindled.
Each day, we left the road
to glean in the fields for leftover crops.
Here and there, we uncovered
a potato, a carrot, a few beets
an overlooked cabbage head.

Once, someone spotted a stray calf.
It was quickly caught and butchered,
the meat distributed,
cooked, and eaten.

Justa's Escape

Now, Willy's tooth ached—
his jaw was swollen with pain.
The other boys tied it to string
to yank it out,
but the root was too deep
and it only made it hurt more intensely—
too much to chew raw carrots,
potatoes or beets
we found in the fields.
And we could not cook them
because we traveled until dark.

Like a miracle,
we got a message
passed from wagon to wagon.
"Look, a factory—
a sugar factory—
in the distance!"
People went running—
and so did Willy—
with buckets, bags, and gunnysacks.
Willy returned lugging a heavy sack.
"It's real sugar, Mama! Ground sugar!"
He hoisted his bag up to the wagon.
"Breakfast, lunch, and dinner all at once!"
He scooped himself a heaping cup of sugar,
and licked it voraciously.
I was used to coarse lumps;
this was fine sugar for the wealthy,
and I had never seen it before.
"I want some, too, Mama" I pleaded.
She dipped a cup into the sack.
We rarely had sugar at home
and now I could eat all I wanted?
But dry sugar soon lost its appeal
before I'd had eaten even half a cup.

XXVIII. The Journey Continues

Willy, though, hadn't eaten for days
and he finished his.

As it began to rain again,
Anna and I huddled
under the tarp
to sleep with Tante and Mama for the night.
The boys lined up under the wagon.
The days added up—
sometimes dreary, sometimes bright,
and growing chillier.
One very cold day near October's end,
snow, then sleet, pelted us.
Franz thought he was old enough to curse.
"*Donner Wetter*," he hissed.
"Franz—your language," Mama warned.
He guided the wagon off the road
and on to the shoulder.
"Prrrrrrrrrrr," he ordered,
and just like that, the horses stopped.
As he jumped to the ground, he muttered.
"Something is wrong!
It's that back left wheel.
It's broken!"

Impatiently, he flung things from the wagon
until he located the spare wheel.
Men came from other wagons to help
and children, in need of entertainment,
crowded around to watch.

The men grunted and strained to lift the heavy wagon,
but their effort was not enough.
Wagons that had been far behind now passed us.
Worried, I chewed my fingers.
What if we're left?

Justa's Escape

What if our people lose us?
Out of nowhere,
several German soldiers appeared
and added their muscle to raise our wagon.
They coaxed the old wheel off;
and slid the new wheel on and locked it in place.
One kind-faced soldier noticed Mama,"
"*Frau*," he said, "there is a soup kitchen ahead,
run by the German Refugee Relief Organization (GRO)—
and there's a barn to spend the night."

Mama beamed in gratitude,
"The Lord bless you."
It was after dark when we arrived at that barn,
and there was barely enough soup left,
a scant cupful each.
Still hungry, I wondered,
would there be room in the barn for us?

The barn was large, but crowded.
I saw no familiar faces.
Had we lost our fellow villagers?
Where would we fit?
Franz scouted out a small open space
where Mama, Tante, Anna, Ben, and I could sleep.
We crowded together on a thin layer of straw.

On the platform above us,
a huge, burly man lay asleep,
snoring more loudly than I had ever heard.
His giant mustache, his long sheepskin coat,
and his black muddy boots—
formed a picture of a scary St. Nicholas.
Franz and Will went off on their assignment—
guarding the wagons for the first half of the night.
"But where will they sleep

when they come in?" I asked Mama.

"God will provide," she assured me.

"Don't forget to pray."

No matter where we were, Mama always said thanks

for the day's blessings.

That day, there were five:

protection from harm,

the extra wheel,

the helpful men,

the hot soup,

and the dry barn.

All that night was strangely quiet,

with no explosions, even distant ones.

I slept soundly

until Mama's shriek awoke me.

She was sitting up, hands to her face,

rocking back and forth, moaning.

Mama was hurt!

Just coming in from his watch,

Franz tried to sort it all out.

It had something to do with the big man.

"There is no room! I didn't see her.

I only turned over," the man groused.

He had stretched out a leg

and kicked Mama hard

just above her right eye.

By morning, her face was puffed up,

one eye swollen shut,

a big, bluish bulge above it.

We stayed another day,

"We need to rest the horses," Franz said.

Mama wanted us to clean ourselves up.

I scratched all the time

and noticed the others did, too.

"We're infested," Mama declared.

Justa's Escape

"With lice."
Disgustedly, Anna added,
"What can we expect?
We haven't washed ourselves
or our clothes in weeks."
Anna was right;
our clothes were stiff and stuck to our bodies.
Mama had me undress
and wrap up in a blanket.
We had no fine-toothed comb,
so she picked through my hair
with her fingers.
She looked along the seams of my dress
and squished the nasty critters
between her thumb nails.
In the meantime, the soup kitchen
had moved on to feed others
so we could choose to be hungry,
roam the village to beg,
or forage in the fields.
Oh, no! Don't make me a beggar!
I prayed silently.
I'd heard a farmer had chased away
Maria Janzen with his pitchfork
when she asked for food.
"You German traitors!" he had shouted,
"you can starve to death."

1. Mennonite Library and Archives Photo Collection. 2005–006. Copyright © Bethel College. Used with permission. https://mla.bethelks.edu/archives/numbered-photos/pholist2.php?num=2005–006

2

2. Mennonite Library and Archives Photo Collection, 2004–141. Copyright © Bethel College. Used with permission. https://mla.bethelks.edu/archives/numbered-photos/pholist2.php?num=2004–141

XXIX. How Can We Go On?

We felt constantly threatened
that the Russian army would catch up
so our caravan could scarcely pause to rest.
The hunger, the cold, and the harsh conditions
brought sickness to babies,
young children, and the elderly.

Some died.
Then we stopped, but only so long
as to wrap the body in a sheet
and dig a shallow grave.
Time enough, only,
for a quick prayer
and a rough cross nailed together,
hurriedly pushed in the soil to mark the spot.
We had to move on.

We had been on the road for two-and-a-half months.
The temperature dropped drastically and stayed there.
Ice thickly glazed the roads.
Horses slipped.
Some broke their legs
and you probably know what happened then.
Our food was gone.
There were no more barns for shelter.
People were losing hope.
How could we go on?

Justa's Escape

Going ahead, our leader
arranged for us to stop
in a Ukrainian village.
The GRO ordered the residents
to take us into their homes.
They assigned us to share
a couple's two-room house.
There, we took turns,
naked under the blanket,
while Mama boiled our clothes
to kill the lice.

For a few weeks,
our whole family slept on the floor
in one small room.
They let Mama cook on their stove.
The war was still on;
we heard it day and night.

Then, the GRO arranged for a cattle train
to carry us west,
farther from the front.
In addition to the seven of us,
forty-five others boarded the boxcar
with all that we carried.
It was very crowded;
the only comfort they provided
was a scattering of straw on the floor
and a slop bucket in the corner
for us to use as a toilet.

"Mama," I worried aloud,
"I'll never be able to go in front of all these people."
Then the train started to move,
although its door remained open.
We children were curious and excited

because it was our first train ride.
Ben leaned out the open door
to try to see the huge locomotive pulling us
and suddenly, without warning,
someone outside slammed the heavy door shut,
knocking him back into the car.

He fell and lay still.
"Oh, God! "Mama cried.
"Water, cold water, please!"
But there was no water.
With the crowd, I watched.
Mama rubbed Ben's head,
making his arms move,
pleading, "wake up, Ben!"
I was of no help to my desperate mother.
Is my brother dead?" I thought.
I remembered how God woke the dead in Bible times.
Could He still do that now?
Finally, with a brief stirring, Ben's eyelids flickered.
He had come back to us,
but he lay quietly for a long while.

Later, when dark had come,
he sat up and vomited and vomited.
Very slowly, he began to talk,
but his words were slurred.
The train jerked with many stops and starts;
eventually we came to Poland.
Now, it was three months since we'd begun.
I could not have imagined that three months would pass
without a real bath,
without brushing my teeth,
and wearing clothes
that were rarely washed.

XXX. The Refugee Camp

In Poland, we learned
we would be taken to a refugee camp.
When we arrived, they said
we needed disinfecting showers.
They separated us,
boys from girls,
men from women.
Everyone, young or old, was made to undress.
Next to me, Elsa whispered,
"I won't take off my underpants."
But the woman in charge saw us.
"*Alles! Alles abziehen!*" she yelled.
The loud woman stormed over
and yanked off Elsa's underwear.
Elsa shrank in embarrassment.

Tante tried to hold onto her kerchief for modesty,
using it to cover herself,
but the bossy woman snatched it away.
"No, no!" You cannot keep that filthy rag!"
I could not meet Tante's eyes
because I felt such shame for her.
They carried all our clothes away;
reassuring us:
"You'll get them back when they are clean."

XXX. The Refugee Camp

Then, like our cows, we were herded,
into a huge shower room—
would we never know privacy?
Afterwards, they gave back our clothes
then steered us through the bitter cold
up to the second level of an empty flour mill.
More and more of us streamed in.
Our count was three-hundred and fifty,
each one claiming a small space
on the floor for us and our meager belongings.
We could use the toilets and sinks on the level below.
Again, we did not undress for the night,
lying down on the straw-strewn floor.

"I'm tired of being so crowded together," Ben griped.
"Just be thankful," Mama reminded us.
"we are out of the cold
and twice a day,
we get parsnip soup and bread."

Mealtime on the trek[1]

1. Mennonite Library and Archives Photo Collection, 2005–007. Copyright © Bethel College. Used with permission. https://mla.bethelks.edu/archives/numbered-photos/pholist2.php?num=2005–007

XXXI. Elsa, Where Are You?

Not since the sanitation showers,
had I seen Elsa.
I had found my village classmates:
Nina, Greta, and Sonya.
Together we searched
up and down the long narrow hallways
between the rows and rows of people,
but Elsa's family seemed to be gone.

Greta spoke like an expert:
"Three hundred and fifty people here—
my brother Martin says—
we just have to look harder."
"Maybe her family already got sent
to live with a Polish family,"
Nina speculated.
"It's just a matter of time
until we're all sent off
to live in different villages."
I did not reply;
all we really wanted
was to go back to our village homes.

We girls had nothing much to do.
It was too cold to play outside
and there were no books to read.
We invented word games,
but argued about the rules.

Almost always, we talked endlessly
about the good times,
all in the past,
so very far away.

Franz announced that the brothers
were going exploring.
"We have nothing to do here;
maybe we can find work in town."
They came back in early evening,
just in time for supper soup.
Flushed with excitement, Franz reported,
"We found the Red Cross office.
They help to find family members.
They have lists of refugees
who crossed into Poland."
"We told them about Papa," Willy said.
"About Hans, Jacob, Gerhard, Dietrich, and Peter,
and then about our nieces and nephew."
Something, maybe hope,
passed over Mama's face.
"Do you think they can find them?"
"We have to hope, Anna," Tante answered.
"We have to pray and hope."

When supper had been cleaned up,
Papa's old friend Peter Rempel stopped by.
"I heard your boys found the Red Cross—
was there any word of Dietrich?"
Mama just shook her head.
"Such a good man," Mr. Rempel added.
"I liked working with him."
He lingered, as if he could not just walk away.
"This winter—" he said,
"they say it is the coldest since Napoleon's march into Russia.
He could not conquer the weather

and he lost the war.
I believe the Germans will also be beaten by the winter."
Was Mr. Rempel just passing time,
like so many of our men
with no work to do?

Young woman on the trek[1]

XXXII. Nina's Secret

After yet another bowl of parsnip soup,
Nina and Greta pulled me away.
"See that woman," Nina gestured
to a woman propped up into a corner,
"with the braid wound around her head?
Mama told me she's about to have a baby.
Look at her big belly.
Her husband is dead from the war."

Greta added,
"I heard the women talking—
Sara is also having a baby."
"Impossible!" I said.
"Sara is only two years older than me.
And besides—she is not married.
She can't have a baby!"
"Justa," Nina whispered urgently,
"you can have a baby without a husband.
Sara's been getting her monthlies."

What are monthlies? I wondered,
but I didn't dare ask,
not wanting to look stupid,
and Nina just went on, unaware.

"Remember when Sara's family wagon got stuck
and German soldiers came to pull them out of the mud?"
"Yes, I remember," I nodded.

"And afterward," Nina continued,
"that soldier walked with Sara,
and held her hand?"

"Is that how you get a baby?" I asked.
"Holding hands?"
Why did Nina and Greta know so much more
when we were all the same age—
thirteen?

XXXIII. Out of the Camp

Franz, in high spirits,
came back from the camp office
with a handful of papers.
We're going!" he announced.
"We're leaving this camp!"

Mama examined the papers.
We had been assigned to a Polish family
in the village of Freihaus.
Although I was glad to be moving on,
the news also hurt;
Nina and Greta would go to a different village.

Gathering our belongings did not take long—
the Singer sewing machine, the Kruger clock—
our bundles of bedding and cookware.
The only clothing we had
was on our backs.

You have only an hour," Mama called,
as I ran off to tell my friends goodbye.
"Justa, will we write?" asks Nina.
We promised,
believing we would somehow find each other.

The transport truck was already nearly full
with two other families and all they owned,
yet we somehow crammed in and slowly pulled away.

Justa's Escape

Several hours later, we shuddered to a stop.
The driver leaned back, announcing,
"Anna Neufeld family!
This house is for you!"

With cramped limbs and ringing ears,
we climbed down, waiting behind
as Mama approached the house.

"Were you expecting us?"
she asked in German of the couple at the door.
They only nodded.
Their silence was awkward.

"May we come in?" Mama finally dared to ask.
The man and woman stepped aside
and all seven of us filed in.
There were two rooms and a kitchen.
One room was completely bare,
so that is where we would sleep.

Several days later,
a woman appeared and registered us
for ration cards to buy food.
"You must take your daughter," she told Mama,
"to enroll in school tomorrow."
Yet another new experience!
"Mama, don't make me go," I pleaded.
I was scared.
How would I even find the school?
I knew no one.
I could not speak Polish.
Surely, the other students would make fun of me.

"Now, Justa," Mama reasoned.
"We'll wash your dress tonight.

XXXIII. Out of the Camp

Tomorrow will be a new day.
We are in occupied Poland.
It is expected to speak German here."
In the morning, I groaned,
pretending my stomach ached,
and somehow, Mama believed me.
I could stay with her one more day.

Finally, some good news;
Big brother Dietrich arrived!
He found us with the help of the Red Cross,
He also brought news of Gerhard's family,
evacuated from Ukraine,
and landing in France.

XXXIV. More Changes

I woke in the thin light of morning,
not feeling well,
both dull and sharp inside,
a warm stickiness between my thighs.
I hurried to the outhouse—
blood.

I breathed deeply,
fought not to faint.
Shaking,
frightened and frozen.
Nothing to wipe myself clean.
I crept to the nearby stream,
just a trickle, really;
I washed myself in its icy water.

"Up so early?" Mama asked
when I returned.
But I was silent.
Could she see I was trembling?
Blood, did this mean I would be having a baby?
I searched my memory;
Have I held hands with a man?
Did I accidentally hold hands
with one of my brothers
when we slept beside each other in those barns?

XXXIV. More Changes

How would my family bear such shame?
I prayed God would let me die
before this baby came.

Finally, morning came.
I must go to school;
Mama would not relent
even though I protested,
"I'm sick, Mama."

On my way to school,
I detoured to the stream.
Finding a rag in the weeds,
I cleaned up again.

It was a one-room school;
When I told the teacher I had finished grade four,
I had to prove myself
by doing math at the blackboard.
My hand quivered as I wrote.
"*Gut!*" the teacher exclaimed,
and put me in grade five.

Relief—
soon spoiled.
Returning to my desk,
again, the warm sticky stuff
oozed down my legs.
Underpants
would have soaked it up,
but mine,
too old and worn to stay up,
were left behind long ago.

My face went stiff,
lifeless.
By now, the blood had soaked through my dress.

Justa's Escape

I had to escape that classroom.
I heard the teacher's voice,
but not her words.

When the recess bell rang,
I waited for the others to scurry out.
Hoping not to be noticed,
I slipped out, ran back to the creek,
washed myself again,
and hid the rag in a tree.

At home that evening,
Dietrich revealed he had two train tickets—
one was for Mama—
to visit Gerhard in France.
"No," she objected,
and we knew she meant it,
"I will never leave the family."
"But, Mama," Dietrich coaxed,
"Gerhard asked for you;
this would help you recuperate from the trek."
"Yes, we all need to recover,
but I refuse to go.
Instead," and Mama looked at me,
"We will send Justa.
Of all of us, she needs to recover most.
She is so skinny:
She is not growing."

I was reassured that Mama would not leave us.
But I—I could not imagine leaving her!
"Justa," Mama said,
"Do you want to go?
You could help to care for Lina.
Your little niece is five now.
You would get better food.

XXXIV. More Changes

Gerhard says they have all they need to eat."
Mama brought this up
as if she'd been considering it for a while.

"For how long," I asked,
"would I be gone?
"About four weeks," Dietrich answered.
"Then I'll come and get you,
or maybe Gerhard will bring you back to Mama."

I shrugged.
I didn't know what to do.
It was a long night
on my narrow pallet on the floor
between Mama and Anna.
Restlessly, I argued with myself,
back and forth
between staying and going.

Leaving might be a way to face my secret—
the baby I knew was growing inside me.
Gerhard's wife, Anya, is a midwife.
She would know how to save the family from this shame.
I would go.
Morning came and I stayed home from school,
wrapped in a blanket
while Mama washed my only dress.

Then, taking her last white pillowcase,
she sewed it into a slip for me.
First, she unraveled some old yellowed lace
to crochet two straps.
She added some of that lace for the hem.
I took off the scratchy wool army blanket slip
for the last time.

XXXV. Awful! Awful!

Despite my brother's urging—
"Justa, we have reserved seats!
You must come in and sit down—."
I had stayed on my feet for two hours.
It won't do for me to sit in the train's coach;
I might bleed through to the seat.
Instead, I stood swaying,
balanced on the platform between cars,
watching the scene pass me by.
Why had I agreed to go with Dietrich to France?
I had been inside—
to the bathroom—
several times,
every time I felt it coming.
By late afternoon, I was faint from hunger,
on my feet all day.

At dusk, we chugged into Berlin.
Dietrich scoured the train schedule.
"We took the wrong train," he muttered,
but it was an easy mistake to make.
The station we wanted—
it had been heavily bombed—
no longer existed.
No night train ran to Thionville,
which was where we wanted to go,
so, we must wait until morning.

XXXV. Awful! Awful!

We went looking for the bomb shelter
to spend the night.
It was empty.
Eerie.
Fluorescent silver walls
made it seem even colder.
It reassured me to see 'Damen',
a bathroom for women.
We staked out spaces
on the long row of hard backless benches
where we could stretch out.
Blessedly, there were no air raids that night.
Only stillness.
Yet, I did not sleep.

At morning's first light,
we found our train and were on our way again.
In a few hours, I hurried to the car's toilet.
Awful!
I saw I had left a visible trail of blood droplets
and I could get no water from the faucet.
How could I clean myself up
and remove the spots from the floor?
Helpless with shame,
I could only shake.
God help me, I pled.
Once more, I retreated to my outside haven.
The conductor, a woman, passed,
entered our car.
She looked at the floor.
She came back outside,
said something questioning,
which I did not catch.
All the while,
She pointed and gestured at me.

Justa's Escape

I felt almost unbearable shame
I pretended not to understand.
Exasperated, she moved on.
Finally, near noon, we arrived at Diedenhofen,
(which is Thionville in French).
We found Anya and Lina at home,
but Gerhard was at work.
"I'm five years old," little Lina boasted.
Anya put out food for us,
the first since we left.
Pre-occupied,
I crossed the kitchen's black and white tile floor,
headed for the bathroom
where I could again struggle.
with my worry and shame.
But Anya interrupted—
"Justa, let me talk to you. "

In no time she was back with water, towel,
white underpants,
and what looked like a little doll pillow.
"Put this in the underwear,"
she said, in a matter-of-fact way.
"You have become a woman now.
All women get this.
You are a woman, now."
She said it, almost joyfully.
I did not fully understand,
but Anya somehow knew.
She was not shaming me.
Why hadn't Mama told me about this?
I was not having a baby.
Of course, I felt relieved;
But I never would have left Mama
had I known.

XXXVI. Letters to Mama

19 May 1944
Dear Mama,

Oh, how I wish you were here with us. We have lots of good food. It is fun to be with little Lina. She is so active all the time. I can't keep up with her!

We speak Russian when we are at home. Anya sends me to market all by myself to get whatever she needs. There, I hear everyone speaking German, even though we are in France. Gerhard says that is because Germany is occupying France.

I have a room on the second floor, and a bed, too, all to myself! There is a large window overlooking Anya's vegetable garden. From that window, I can see the cemetery. Each morning, a mother and two girls dressed in black pass by carrying flowers. I can see a church with a tall steeple. Every day the bells ring.

When I first arrived, Anya washed my hair in kerosene to get rid of the lice. Then she boiled my clothes.

Right now, Lina has been waiting, not so patiently, for me to take her outside to play, so I must go.

Auf Wiedersehen!
Justa

16 July 1944
Dear Mama,

Today is my fourteenth birthday. Did you remember? Nobody here mentioned it until I told Lina and she told Anya. So, they took me to the park by the River Moselle. Anya gave me a little notebook. I will write in it as a daybook so someday I can share what has happened while we are apart. Anya bought us a sweet pastry that was very good. I told her that at home, the birthday girl would be sitting on a pillow at the supper table. She laughed because she had never heard that before and she said that her Ukrainian customs are different from our German ways.

Mama, you wrote that since the boys are German citizens now that the government could send them to fight at the front. I hope not! Since Dietrich has an office job as an interpreter, maybe Franz, Will, and Ben could help him.

Gerhard has a friend, Alex, who is also an engineer and they work in the same factory together. He and his wife are also from Ukraine. Gerhard and Alex always talk about the war. They sound as if they are scared Germany is going to lose. They always end up by saying, "What is going to happen to us, then?"

Mama, yesterday I met a girl named Etta who is one year older than me. She has a sister, Marusja. They are also from Ukraine. Marusja also works in a factory. I hope I can see Etta often because I miss Elsa and Nina so much. If you see them, tell them to write to me.

Yes, I say my prayers every night.

Auf wiedersehen,
With love, Justa.

10 August 1944
Dear Mama,

I worry because you have not answered my last three letters. Every day, I wait for the postman, but he just walks right by our house. Anya is also looking for letters from her friend in Poland and she does not hear from her, either. Have you moved? Is it possible you have all gone back home?

I can tell that Gerhard and Anya are very worried about what will happen to us. Gerhard tells us that the Russian Army is now in Poland and that they might send you back to Ukraine. I wish I was there with you. Here, no one from Ukraine wants to go home. They are afraid they would really be sent to Siberia to the labor camps.

Twice a week, I go to Madam Henkel's house to help her with cleaning. She is our neighbor. Her house never seems dirty, but she has me mostly dusting in one room that she calls her museum. She has shelves of glass and porcelain figurines. Anya says that Madam Henkel is a countess related to Alexander, the last Czar of Russia.

What do you and Tante do? What is Anna's work and does she like it?

Mama, write soon—right away! I am so homesick.

Auf weidersehen,
Justa

14 August 1944
Mama,

Where are you? I am so worried. Please answer me

Justa

XXXVII. Tagebuch (Daybook), Part One; The Americans

14 August 1944

Gerhard and his friend Alex
stay up late with the radio.
It is all about the war.
Gerhard predicts
the Americans will soon be here
to occupy France.
We think Mama is in Poland—
one month without hearing from her—
He doubts she gets my letters.
I miss her most at night.
No one knows I cry—
My pillow is still wet by morning.
I wish I had not left her.

15 August 1944
Still no letter from Mama.
What if we never find each other?
What if she has died in the war?
Then we'll meet again in heaven.
We are crazy-worried.
What will the Americans do when they come?
Will they force us back to Russia?
Will they hold it against us
that we are German?

XXXVII. Tagebuch (Daybook), Part One; The Americans

Each week holds one bright spot—
I stop thinking of Mama
when I earn a few francs
from Madam Henkel.
I dust her pretty collection
of priceless things.
She praises me
because I am so careful.
"Stay for tea," she coaxes.
In her sitting room,
she sets out a silver platter,
silver spoons,
sugar cubes in a bowl,
and a pot of strawberry jam.
She urges me to take sugar,
insists on big spoons full of jam.
And then we visit,
as if I am a grownup, too.

30 August 1944
Infrequently,
because she works with a family,
I get to see my friend Etta.
I do not envy her
because it would be painful—
being around children—
I can feel the worry in our house.
Gerhard is even more quiet.
Anya says, "I will die here
rather than go back to communism."
And this talk of dying
makes me think of Mama.
Does she still live?
Does God even hear my prayers?
Is He even there?

Justa's Escape

1 September 1944
All week,
Gerhard has said,
"the Americans are coming."
Today, he came home early from the factory.
The German supervisors had run away.
Desperate hooligans broke in,
looted anything they could carry.
Dusk brought military vehicles
to our neighborhood.
Through the streets,
Happy people ran,
waving flags,
shouting in French.
A large covered truck
stopped in front of our house.
A man in uniform stepped out.
His skin was very dark—
He had been almost invisible
inside the shadowed truck!
I held back,
But Gerhard and Anya were bolder—
They even smiled.
"These are the Americans!"
Gerhard exclaimed.

2 September 1944
Anya sent me to the market
to buy milk.
Everyone spoke French openly;
They flew their flags everywhere.
The mood was happy and loud.
I wanted that joy, too,
but instead,
I thought about Mama, Tante, and Anna;
We still do not know where they might be.

XXXVII. Tagebuch (Daybook), Part One; The Americans

Earlier, I had guessed they might be with the Americans.
I asked Gerhard if that is where they were.
"No, Justa", Gerhard said,
with no reassurance.
"By now,
they are in the clutches of the Red Army."
I shivered at his words,
but still,
I wished I were with them.

3 September 1944
Today, I worked for Madam Henkel.
She was also happy
the Americans had come,
because she is married to an American
and she wants to be taken to America.
"I have uncles in Canada," I said,
but we have not been allowed to contact them
for many years."
"But, now, "Madam Henkel said,
"at least you could write to them again."
Later, that gave Gerhard an idea.
"I'll write to Uncle Ben
through the Red Cross.
Maybe they can find our family."
I still had hope,
but I also had doubt—
It floated deep in my throat like a big bubble,
but I swallowed my question.
What if the Red Cross sent bad news?

5 September 1944
We still needed ration cards to buy anything,
but Gerhard is afraid
to register us for them
because he doesn't trust the Russians.

Even though the Americans and Russians
are fighting on the same side,
they might use the registry
to find out we are here.
"If they know we are hiding in France,"
Anya fretted,
"they'd call us traitors for leaving Ukraine
and they'd send us to Siberia."
It was all so confusing—
hard to know who to trust.
The Americans were kind to us.
When we were hungry,
soldiers Richard and Charley
brought us leftovers from their kitchen
to keep us from starving.
Richard gave Anya two army blankets.
She would have one dyed
and sewed into an overcoat for me.
They also left me a pair of soldier's shoes.

XXXVIII. Tagebuch, Part Two; Fear and Waiting

7 November 1944
For a long while,
I have not had the courage to write.
Something happened to me
which I have tried to forget.
Maybe an angel protected me.
It was already dusk.
I had just parted from Etta
and turned the corner into the alley
where our house stood.
And then I heard my name.
"Justa." It was Charley,
the good doctor.
Yesterday, he'd noticed
my festering finger.
"She'll lose that finger,"
he said, "or maybe her arm
if the infection is not drained."
So, I agreed
and he made a cut
to relieve the swelling.
Now, I could feel
my bandaged finger already healing.
Motioning me closer
Charley held out a chocolate bar.
When I reached out,
he grabbed me.
His breath smelled of alcohol.

Justa's Escape

He embraced me—
perhaps too tightly—
rubbed me—
Hugs used to feel good,
but this one frightened me.
Then he pulled up my skirt.
My struggles—
my pleas to God—
had no effect.

Then I heard Anya:
"Justa! Justa! Come home!"
Something changed in Charley's face.
Releasing his grip,
he shoved me away.
I stumbled into the alley,
recovered my steps
and dashed home.
Anya swept me inside.
Her face was stern
and she was shaking.
When alone,
I collapsed onto my bed.
Trembling and sobbing,
waves of rage, guilt, and relief
moved through me.
How could this be my fault?
How could Anya blame me?

10 June 1945
So much has happened to us.
We are hiding in a village
so I must not write its name.
It began at the train station
where I was meeting Madam Henkel
as she came home from Paris.

A friendly man stopped me
to admire my hair.
He was French,
But his Russian was good.
"You have beautiful braids,
the way you wrap them
atop your head," he said.
"And you don't look French.
Where are you from?"
Politely, I answered all his questions—
my name—
where I was from—
my brother's name—
our address.
"Well," he said,
"you must come with me
to Russian headquarters.
We can help you to return."
Then it dawned on me.
I was in trouble.
He nodded to the men behind him.
"Take this Russian girl to headquarters
while I go to pick up the brother's family."
Three men walked with me—
one on either side
and one behind me.
My heart pounded.
My friendliness had got me into this.
At headquarters,
a Russian soldier peppered me with questions.
"So," he concluded,
"you go home on the next train.
You know your mother
is there waiting for you."
Could this be? I wondered,
worry just beneath my hope.

Justa's Escape

How would Gerhard and Anya react?
They trusted me to keep our lives secret.
Suddenly,
the friendly man burst through the doors.
"Why did you tell me all those stories?"
he demanded of me.
Then he and soldier argued loudly.
Then the man grabbed my arm
and half-dragged me home
to where my brother waited.
Nervously, Gerhard held out a small package
which the man took and hurried away.
Gerhard sighed heavily.
"Quickly pack your things.
We must leave immediately."
It seems the French man
secretly worked for the Russians.
Since that day,
we have been in hiding,
arranged by friends of friends.

1 July 1945
Yes, we are still living in secret,
seldom going outside.
Nobody but our hosts must know we are here.
At night, Gerhard sneaks out to check the mailbox.
He looks for a letter from Uncle Ben in Canada.
Yesterday, Anya asked me,
"Do you know what you are worth?"
She answered her own question:
"Three packs of American cigarettes!
That is what Gerhard had to pay
to buy you from the Russians."

XXXIX. Tagebuch (Daybook), Part Three; Was It God?

16 July 1945
Today is my fifteenth birthday,
and more than a year since I last saw Mama.
but we are back in an apartment,
although we must keep the shutters closed
all the time
and pretend no one lives here.
We still fear the Russians.
If they find us,
we will be sent to a labor camp in Siberia.
"because," Gerard said,
"President Roosevelt,
Prime Minister Churchill,
and General Secretary Stalin
agreed that all Russian refugees
should be repatriated."
Now, we are so rich!
We get care packages from America—
big cardboard boxes full of a meat called *Spam*,
steak and kidneys,
liver loaf, bacon,
and something yellow—
margarine—
a spread like butter—
lard, honey, sugar, and coffee.
These care packages keep us alive.

Justa's Escape

Some of it we trade on the Black Market
for clothing and things we need.

1 September 1945
God, I am afraid to ask,
but I am wondering.
Do you exist?
Are you even real?
I need for you to show me a sign.
I am pleading.

I was coming home from the market—
Anya had sent me to fetch milk –
but with no ration cards
I was returning empty-handed.
Then, there on the streetcar,
someone tapped my shoulder.
It was the Russian officer
who had interrogated me
and prepared papers
to send me back to Russia.
"So, you are still here."
he said, flatly.
"We can make room for you
on the next train."
I jumped from the streetcar before it stopped.
I ran, nearly breathless.
As I fled, I wound my way home,
weaving in unnecessary turns
in case the Russian had followed.
As I looked back,
I did not see him,
but I was not reassured.
I prayed,
"God, I need you.
Help us now

so I can know you exist."
Something was odd.
Before our apartment,
a strange vehicle stood.
I shivered.
Could the Russians already be there
to drag us to the train station?
Should I escape?
But where would I go?
I hesitated,
but knew I must go inside.
I could not abandon my brother's family
just to save myself.
Without them,
I am even more alone in the world.

I crept past the car.
On its door was a painted picture,
a circle enclosed a handshake,
arced with letters spelling
CANADA.
Surely, these are not Russians!
Has Uncle Ben come from Canada to rescue us?
I leapt up the stairs,
two-at-a time;
our apartment door stood ajar.
There I saw a man,
speaking Low German,
the language I knew best.
Could this be God himself?
Had he heard my prayer, after all?
No, the man was not God.
I soon learned his name,
Peter Dyck, a refugee worker,
sent from Canada to help us.
Anya and Gerhard deliberated;

we hurriedly packed what we could carry
and piled into Mr. Dyck's automobile.

28 September 1945
Belgium
Miracles!
Thank-you, God!
I believe you exist.
Mr. Dyck had come to rescue us.
We had no passports,
but his Canadian documents were good enough.
They got us through the border checkpoints.
"I'm giving these refugees a lift,"
was all he had to say.
They waved us on.
Tonight, we sleep in Belgium.
"Tomorrow, you will be in Holland,"
Mr. Dyck said.
"The Dutch will not let the Russians
take you back against your will.
You will be safe there".
Safety!
I could almost feel the burden lift.
No more looking over my shoulder;
no more worry,
of someone coming after me.

XL. Tagebuch, Part Four; The Netherlands

1 October 1945
Two days after leaving France,
we arrived at Holland's border.
I thought trouble was behind us,
but at the checkpoint
that familiar fear returned.
We waited in the car
While Mr. Dyck negotiated.
He paced back and forth.
"No visas, no entry,"
Gerhard whispered.
Many minutes passed.
At last, we saw the officer
in the booth on the telephone.
Soon, Mr. Dyck strolled back to us
and we were on our way again.

We are in Holland now.
Now, we stay in one of many cabins
in the woods in *Fredeshiem,*
a Dutch Mennonite retreat center.
Ukrainian Mennonite Refugees—
233 in all—joined us
I feel comforted:
I am surrounded
by speakers of *Plautdietsch;*
simple and plentiful meals;
and encircled by tall old trees.

Justa's Escape

Now I must get used to not being afraid—
accustomed to being happy.
Other girls my age—
some also separated from their families
—are here, too.
Annie is especially friendly to me;
I remind her of her missing younger sister.
"May I call you little *Schwesterlein?*" she asked.
"Oh, yes! I also miss my sister," I answered.
Annie told me all girls—
fifteen and older—
will work as housemaids in Amsterdam.
I am still a minor,
so I would need Gerhard's permission.
"Bah!" I scoffed.
"I am not going to ask him.

I am fifteen!
That is old enough to do as I want.
From now on,
I will be on my own!"

15 November 1945
Amsterdam
Here we are in Amsterdam,
the Netherland's capital city.
Another refugee girl, Lenie,
and I share a room in a pastors' home.
We have been assigned to work
at separate houses
not far from each other.
Lenie is a maid in that home.
I work for a family.
Mr. G. is a pastor and university professor.
The mother is in a wheelchair;
her legs are covered in sores.

XL. *Tagebuch, Part Four; The Netherlands*

They have two older sons
and a daughter,
Williementje,
just ten years old.
I like her already.
Dutch sounds almost like our Plautdietsch,
but just to be sure I understand,
Mrs. G. gives me directions in German.

30 November 1945
Amsterdam
Two weeks have passed
since ten refugees,
ten men and twenty girls,
moved here from Fredesheim.
The men came to help distribute clothing and food.
Most of the girls—except for me—
already know them from a camp
where they were together.
They invited us to visit them on Sundays.
That is where Peter Dyck,
our rescuer,
lives with his wife, Elfrieda.
She is like a mother to us,
wanting to know how we are getting along—
what it is like to work as maids.
She welcomes our questions.
She encourages us to sing songs from home.
Elfrieda asks someone to read from the Bible,
and then she prays with us.
Before we head home,
she serves tea and cookies.
I can't imagine where she gets them.
Since the war, the stores have none.

Justa's Escape

6 January 1946
Amsterdam
Last Wednesday, our afternoon off,
Lenie and I went to the MCC house.
We met the new relief workers—
Marie and Magdalene—
from America.
They joined us in singing.
We felt we had known them for a long time.
Magdalene Friesen speaks Plautdietsch.
I called her Fraulein Friesen.
She laughed.
"Call me Maggie!"
We share the same birthdate.
She has only one brother and no sisters.
These Americans are so friendly,
ready to be family.
"Would you like to be my new little sister?"
I nodded, "yes."

She volunteered to tutor me in English.
"You'll need it," she said.
"I am working through the Red Cross
to arrange for a passport
for you
to go to America,
or maybe even to Canada,
to live with your relatives."
I was so excited;
I wanted to tell Gerhard right away.

Every Sunday afternoon
we go to see the young single men.
Henry plays the guitar.
We sing songs we learned in school.
We play games.

We laugh a lot.
I whispered to Lenie,
"Why does Victor look at me all the time?"
"He likes you, silly," Lenie giggled.
Suddenly, as if he had heard,
Victor stood up.
"You wanted to learn to ride a bicycle," he said.
"I will teach you.
My bike is outside."
I flushed red—stammered.
Too shy.
What could I do?
But Elfrieda Dyck rescued me
from my embarrassment.
"I have something to ask you, Justie"—
I liked that she called me that—

"With all these guests,
I need someone in the kitchen
and to do other housework.
How would you like to help me?"
"You mean every day?"
"Yes, every day."
I almost leapt at the offer.
Then I hesitated.
"If the Golterman family will allow it."
Maybe I was too eager.
Could I really cook for all those people—
twenty or more American relief workers?
But I do know how to clean house.
I had learned a lot from Madame Henkel.

27 January 1946
Amsterdam
Yesterday, we girls went along
to take food to the Rovererstein Refugee Camp

where Gerhard, Anya, and Lina are staying.
Maggie told Gerhard about her new plan
to send me to stay with her parents in America.
My brother looked surprised,
but not very enthusiastic.
"You're my responsibility, Justa,"
Gerhard said, very seriously.
He turned to me,
"You can go to America,
but only if Anya, Lina, and I go, also."
Maggie was quick to answer,
"I can arrange that."
Gerhard has been corresponding
with the Red Cross
to find the rest of our family.
He also wrote to Uncle Ben in Canada,
But so far, no word from either Mama or Papa,

The camp is very crowded
More people arrive every day;
as of yet, we saw no one
from our family or the village.
The women stay all together
in just a couple of rooms.
One room is just for mothers and children.
I am lucky to get to live in the big MCC house.

sharing a third-floor room
with just Lenie and Annie.
Gerhard and another refugee teach the camp's children.
The women take turns cooking the meals.
We ate a delicious lunch that made me homesick—
borscht and zweibach.

XLI. Tagebuch, Part Five: Mama Is Alive!

27 February 1947
Amsterdam
Yes, Mama lives!
At least, we know she was alive
six months ago.
That is how long the letter traveled
which she wrote to Uncle Ben.
Our uncle sent it to on to Gerhard
and now I have it.
You know I have prayed,
waiting for this news every day.
When I saw her handwriting
and held the envelope,
my throat went dry.
At first, I could not read it.
At last, I cried and cried.
"Thank-you, God! Thank-you, God!"
I breathed.
Mama and Anna had survived.
But Tante?
My dear Tante was dead.
Starved to death—
are any other words so ugly?
An emptiness opened in me.
When the war had ended,
they were forced into cattle cars,
and shipped to the northern Urals,

where it is bitterly cold.
How are we going to survive here?
Mama wrote.
Desperate,
she traded her sewing machine
and the family clock
for food.
All we have left to trade,
she wrote,
are the clothes off our backs.
Also: *Brother Hans is alive—*
in exile in Kazakhstan.
But where is my husband
and my other seven sons
and my little girl, Justa?
Yes, we are alive,
but I do not know how
Anna and I are going to survive.
It seems, no sooner does God answer,
than I face another question.
"Shall I come to you, Mama?"
I want to ask.
"Shall we die together?"

30 March 1947
Amsterdam
Today I sent Mama a food package.
I enclosed a letter inside.
Gerhard saw me looking at the parcel
He read my eyes.
"Don't ever—
no, never—
think of going back to Russia.
You would not survive a month!
I know he is right,
but to be with Mama—

would that be so bad?
But there was no time
to worry about where I would go.
Maggie burst into the kitchen.
"Your papers came through!"
"If we can book passage on the ship,
you will be in America by Christmas!"
The excitement made me feel
my throat was closing,
limiting my breath.

My words could not get out.
I wanted to say,
"What about Mama?
Can I put the ocean between us?
Will I ever see her again?"
Then the tears came—a stream.
Maggie wrapped me in her arms.
"So happy, huh?"
Not happy!
I broke from her embrace,
fled up the three flights of stairs,
to my room.
where a different set of arms—
Annie's—
comforted me.
She hummed a familiar tune:
"*Take thou my hand, oh Father,
and lead thou me,*"
the hymn Mama and Tante had sung
in our warm kitchen
in the evenings.

13 October 1947
Amsterdam
When I write that

it has all happened so fast,
you might wonder
how I could think that.
I lived these last seven months
in the security of the big house,
always with people
coming and going,
hoping against hope
for all the fragments of our family
to come back together.
miraculously.
But of course,
inside I knew the truth—
in this wounded world,
I was not being realistic.
At last, one day
Maggie called me into her office.
"Justa, your tickets have come.
Here"—
she handed me a wooden suitcase—
"I had this made for you.
Go pack your clothing."
Too stunned to thank her,
I took the painted green suitcase
and numbly turned away.
"Next week."
she called after me,
"is when you are leaving!"
Can you imagine how I felt?
Such a mix of emotions.
Eager to see more of the world.
Ecstatic
at riding on the ocean
in a gigantic ship.
Fearful.
even farther from Mama.

XLI. Tagebuch, Part Five: Mama Is Alive!

Despairing,
never re-assembling
those pieces of my dear family,
scattered over Europe and Asia.

The next day,
Maggie took me shopping.
"You've outgrown your shoes," she said.
"They must be warm enough
for Minnesota winter."
I was elated!
New shoes—
the first pair not hand-me-downs
I had ever owned.
I packed that evening.
I laid my modest wardrobe on the bed—-
just three dresses;
there lay the white slip Mama made—
it was now too small,
and I ached just to see it there—
so simple, so beautiful,
so full of Mama's love.
I could not leave it behind.
There, too, were my two aprons,
my underwear,
and the suit Ava helped me to sew.
And also, the daybook,
and the Bible the Dycks gave me.

XLII. Tagebuch, Part Six; The Ship

21 October 1947
On Board the SS Marine Marlin
Lenie, Annie, and Maggie
and ten others
Came to the docks to say farewell
as I left Amsterdam.
We three girls were soon sobbing.
"Justa, "Lenie cried, "
"promise you will write from America."
Just one more hug.
Just one more kiss.
Finally, we had to let go.

Our boat is a huge troop ship.
It has four decks.
Cabin C 57 is ours—
women and children.
The men stay below.
Seven of us,
the group from Camp Fredeshiem,
are sailing for America.
We hear other languages.
I recognize French, Dutch, and English,
which we—with many other passengers—
do not speak.
We do catch Russian announcements
about the weather we are sailing into.
They update us on the distance

we have traveled so far.
I have had some simple lessons,
but soon, I know,
I will really have to learn English.

25 October 1947
On board the SS *Marine Marlin*
The ship rocks so heavily.
I must hold on to something
in order to walk.
Sick people line up
to bend over the railing.
When I go to the dining room,
people are scarce.
What a shame!
The food is so good.
This must be what heaven is like.
We can eat all the bread we want.
There are no limits to the coffee and milk.
Anya and Lina stay away from the dining room.
They are too seasick.

26 October 1947
On board the SS *Marine Marlin*
The Atlantic Ocean
It is day six.
As far as we can see,
the ocean is all around us.
Suddenly, the ship goes quiet.
The engines have stopped.
"Defective machinery!" someone shouts.
People cluster together, whispering.
Some wear fear on their faces,
but I feel unusually calm.
Resigned,
I am tired of fear and worry;

Justa's Escape

I resolve to be optimistic.
All this traveling
has brought us this far.
Surely, we will make it.
Hours later, we heard,
"the motor has been repaired."
Passengers cheered.
Some even grabbed the nearest person
and started to dance.
The ship rocked with the waves.
The dancers fell into each others' arms.
Propping each other up,
laughing.
I recognized my happiness and relief.
No one chose me to dance,
but I repeated to nobody in particular
"We're moving. We're moving."

Today was Anya's 33rd birthday.
Gerhard had bought her gifts—
an apple and some chocolates.
A seven-year-old Dutch boy
also had a birthday to celebrate.
The chief steward brought a large cake
and some ice cream
into the women's and children's dining room
The youngest ones got stuffed animals.
Soon, amid all the joy,
we recognized violent waves
pitching the boat as if it were a duck.

31 October 1947
Far West Atlantic Ocean
Rumors make the rounds.
We'll dock in New York tomorrow—
One day earlier than expected.

XLII. Tagebuch, Part Six; The Ship

I've been practicing my English,
Repeating,
When we get to Minnesota,
I can say,
"How do you do, Mr. Friesen?"
"How do you do, Mrs. Friesen?"
I try not to worry.
Will there be someone to meet us
When we land?

Saturday
1 November 1947
Today I think of Papa.
It is his birthday
One day,
maybe, he will read this.

Where are you, Papa?
I miss you now
as much as the day
you disappeared.
You would be happy
with us on this ship,
getting closer to Canada,
to Uncle Ben.

Last night,
I hardly slept—
so much uncertainty—
so many questions.
What will America be like?
Will the people be kind?
Will they let me finish school?
Maggie said I could—
that 17 is not too old.

Justa's Escape

They made an announcement:
Breakfast served early—
Landing—
almost a day ahead of time.
Shuffling feet—
Excited conversations.
On *the Marine* deck,
people gathered,
shading their eyes with their hands.
and pointing.
"There! There she is!"
I, too, spotted her.
In the distance,
the statue,
the lady with the torch.

A man in uniform announced
how we would disembark.
"US citizens will leave first.
Next are the British.
Then the French.
Then all others—
that would be our group of seven.

XLIII. Tagebuch, Part Seven; We Arrive

At noon, we reached port.
Immigration officers boarded.
Where was the Mennonite agent
who was to meet us?
One, two, three hours passed,
but no one came.
Were we forgotten—
unwanted?
How long could we linger
on *the Marlin*?
Would we have to sleep on the dock?

Though nervous,
Gerhard took action.
He settled us on a bench
and hurried off to find a telephone.
Sleepy Lina curled up against me.
"Tell me a story, Justa,"
She whimpered,
But anxious,
I was in no mood
for telling stories.

I spied a woman on an opposite bench.
She seemed to be staring—
eavesdropping.
"Where are you from?" she asked.

Justa's Escape

"From Holland."
I answered.
She seemed friendly.
Her clothes were nice,
like Madame Henkel's.
Starting such an ordinary conversation
seemed to relax me,
made me realize
we would be all right.
We had enough experience
to solve these problems.
Even if we had been abandoned,
we could cope.
Soon my brother strolled back;
Just then, we heard his name:
"Gerhard Neufeld—
calling Gerhard Neufeld.
Telephone call."
So Gerhard hurried away,
soon returning,
all smiles.
"They were not expecting us today.
We have an address in the city
Where we can spend the night."

Porters helped to load
our baggage into a taxi station wagon.
In a short time,
we pulled up to 235 East 49th Street.
We piled our bundles,
boxes, and suitcases
on the sidewalk.
The driver demanded twelve dollars.
To us, new immigrants,
it seemed an immense sum;
we had to pool our money.

XLIII. Tagebuch, Part Seven; We Arrive

We dug deep.
I added my precious coins,
which Mr. Brenneman,
an American visitor to the house in Amsterdam
had given me.

We were still short*,
but Gerhard handed over what we had.
The driver frowned,
mumbled something,
threw up his hands,
and shouted something
in a language I could not understand
Finally, he shrugged and grumbled,
"okay!'
slammed the door,
and sped off.

A cluster of people
observed from the stoop
of the tall brick building.
They came towards us, smiling.
One man asked, in Plautdietsch,
"Are you the group from Holland?"*

"Ja!" I answer eagerly.
It turned out that they were Mennonite students
at this seminary.
The MCC agents had planned to meet our ship tomorrow,
so it was up to these young men
to look after us for the night.
"Tomorrow," one explained,
"you'll ride the train to Lancaster."

* equivalent to about $149 in 2022.

Justa's Escape

They walked us to a small diner.
"Try the hamburgers,"
they urged.
"We know Hamburg city in Germany," Gerhard said.
"But what are hamburgers?"
Now, I thought, was my time to show off.
"Something you eat," I boasted.
"Meat atop small round bread—
covered by another small round bread. "
I felt superior because I had cooked this
for Americans in the Amsterdam house.
My confidence swelled,
and I felt hopeful.
Sitting at the small busy tables
in this bright space,
with students and waitresses chattering,
I found I understood snatches of English.
Maybe I could survive in this strange place.

In the morning,
a student led our group to Grand Central Station.
Soon we left for Pennsylvania
and in just a few hours,
MCC staff met us in Lancaster,
and greeted us warmly.
We stayed just one night.
We bade farewell to the Arendt family.
They would ride the train
many miles west to Washington,
where their relatives waited.
Then, it was our turn.
We departed for Minnesota
The train gently rocked;
and we dozed the night away.
I dreamed about Elsa, Nina, and Greta
in a large circle of girls

on the village school playground
playing drop the handkerchief.
It was a dream,
because we were carefree and happy.

The train stopped suddenly,
thrusting me forward.
This was Chicago,
time to change to the *Empire Builder 400*.
Today we would reach our new home—
it had been decided we would stay in Minnesota
instead of joining Uncle Ben.
Canada was not taking refugees.
Getting closer,
I thought about how my life would be.
Who would meet us in Minnesota?
Would the Friesens like me?
Would I be able to finish school?
Would my English be good enough?
Just after midnight,
the conductor called out the next stop.
Mankato!
That was us!
We gathered our belongings
and lurched toward the car's end.
Lina and I tried to peer out
at our new home,
but the land was completely dark.
The platform seemed deserted.
"I don't want to go out into the black night!"
Lina whimpered.
I tried to look brave for Lina's sake,
but my throat had tightened;
my heart thumped wildly.
What if no one had come for us?
But out there was a dim light,

and in the shadows,
several figures huddled together
under umbrellas.

We struggled with our bundles
and stepped out on to the platform.
The small group—
three men and one very tall woman—
approached us.
"I am A. A. Penner,"
one man boomed.
Another shook Gerhard's hand.
"And this is my son-in-law,
Henry Pankratz.
We came in two cars
To have room for your baggage."
Then a short, white-haired, grandfatherly man
spoke up in Plautdietsch
"You must be Justina."
He offered his hand.
"I am Maggie's father.
This is her mother."
He meant the tall woman.
Instantly, I forgot all my English practice
And fell right into familiar Plautdietsch.
Gerhard's little family got into Mr. Penner's car.
Mr. Pankratz took the bags in his car.
My suitcase and I—
we went home with the Friesens.
In just about an hour
we turned down the lane
to a little farmhouse.
"Here we are,"
Mrs. Friesen spoke.
"Welcome to your new home!"

XLIV. Home?

I had a room all to myself
on the second floor
with a closet
big enough to walk into.
I had a dresser, a bookshelf,
and a small table and chair
in front of a big mirror on the wall.
Yes, all to myself!
"Here," Mrs. Friesen said, "
you can sit in front of the mirror
and brush your long lovely hair."

At breakfast, Mr. Friesen said,
"Maggie says to enroll you in school as soon as possible."
I was so excited, but also a bit scared.
I had lost four years of school while we wandered.
"Do you want to go to school?" he asked.
"Oh, yes, Mr. Friesen! Very much.
Will I be able to take a job somewhere at the same time?"
"First of all," he replied,
"you needn't call me Mr. Friesen.
We want you to call us Uncle John and Aunt Mary."

XLV. A New School

Uncle John drove me to Mountain Lake—
I saw the lake,
but will have to ask about the mountain—
eight miles from the farm
to meet with Mr. Klaassen, school principal.
Mr. K., as he wanted me to call him,
could understand when he heard Plautdietsch,
but he spoke only English.
"We will have to test you
to determine what grade to start you in.
I'd like to do that before Christmas
so you can be in school when 1948 begins.
Mr. K's face was stern and scary,
but I felt too happy to be unnerved.
He did not think me too old for school.
"You've probably already had geography.
Tomorrow we'll test in math and English."
After I had taken the tests,
I was not so confident.
I felt like hiding.
I made some errors on the math section.
I was sure my half-page of written English was a disaster.

Several days later, Principal Klaassen telephoned Uncle John.
His news was not all bad.
I could join grade seven after Christmas.
My math was on an eighth-grade level,

XLV. A New School

but he called my English *inadequate*.
"There are several students in grade seven
and they, too, speak Plautdietsch—
they'll help you understand the assignments,"
Uncle John reported.

XLVI. Minnesota: Pure White Outside; Deep Dark Inside

Snow, snow, and more snow.
It kept falling for three days.
No traffic passed by on the highway
on the other side of the fence.
The heavy silence was interrupted only
when Uncle John shoveled a path to the barn.
"The cows must be fed and milked;
the chickens need water and feed."
From my upstairs window
I saw the snow drift up to the garage roof.

Inside, a warm coziness comforted us.
We had food to last the winter—
cupboards full, basement shelves heavy with jars,
bright with fruit and vegetables.
Always, though, far off cold Northern Russia
occupied my thoughts.
In Borowsk, Barrack 17, in the deep forests of the Urals,
Mama and my sister Anna
struggled to survive.
In her last letter, Mama wrote,
First, we traded the family Krueger clock,
and finally the sewing machine
for a few loaves of bread.
Now, there is nothing left to trade.
Anna and her friend Maria are assigned

XLVI. Minnesota: Pure White Outside; Deep Dark Inside

to cut down trees with a handsaw.
If they meet their quota,
each will get 300 grams of bread.
Anna shares her portion with me,
But for her hard labor,
she really needs all of it herself.
Anna is already so frail.
How much longer can she keep working?

As I nestled in this warm house
surrounded by people who cared about me,
I was sometimes overcome by guilt.
How did I earn this life
when others suffer so?
I could not hold back the flood.
My chest heaved;
soon tears flowed.
My eyes were red—
my face must have been swollen.
I could not let the Friesens see me like this.
When Aunt Mary called me for the evening meal,
I replied that I was not hungry,
that I wanted to finish the letter I was writing;
I would soon be down to wash the supper dishes.
But Aunt Mary did not believe me
I heard her footsteps on the stairs.
She found me, covering my face,
crying into the slip Mama sewed for me.
My sobs soon turned into wails.
I sensed Aunt Mary standing there,
not knowing how to respond—
as Maggie's stepmother,
she had never had her own children—
she put a hesitant arm around me,
sat down on the bed beside me.
But I did not feel comforted.

I managed to choke out my words,
"I miss my mother so."

Sometimes I rode along to town with Uncle John
to pick up the mail.
People seemed to stare at me
when they passed us on the sidewalk.
Was it so obvious?
Did I look so different, so strange?
I announced to Uncle John
that I would cut off my long thick braids.
Uncle John looked shocked.
"Oh, no! Don't do that!
You look so wholesome, so natural!"
In the three weeks since I had been in Minnesota,
the Friesens and I had been invited out for meals and coffee
two or three times a week.
Their family and friends wanted to meet me.
We always visited with old people
who had many questions for me.
"We want to hear your story," they insisted.
My story, I wondered.
What is my story?
And their questions piled up,
one on another
like the Mountain Lake snow.
"We have not had any refugees in twenty years,"
Uncle John tried to explain.
"People want to know about you."
They asked questions about life in Ukraine
and our long trek during the war.
but I wanted to forget the war,
to erase what has happened.
But, the old folks,
with their coffee
and their plates of *platzs* and *zweibach*,

XLVI. Minnesota: Pure White Outside; Deep Dark Inside

were nice and kind
so I was polite
and tried to answer the best I knew how.

On one ride home, I wondered out loud,
"Where are all the young people?"
"You'll see them when we go to church
and after Christmas when school begins,"
Aunt Mary answered.

Christmas came and, believe me,
I was glad when it went.
I got too many presents—
a warm scarf, mittens,
overshoes,
a box of writing paper,
envelopes,
and a diary—
more than a lifetime of Christmases.
It was generous,
but it felt so awkward.

With school starting soon,
Uncle John felt I should be closer to town.
He arranged a place for me to stay on weekdays,
a room in a home in Mountain Lake.
"Don't worry," he said,
"you are still welcome at the farm on weekends."
The Pankratz family invited us for dinner
so we could meet.
I was happy to see they had children.
First was Lenore, four years younger.
Then came Stanley and Louise.
Last was baby Barbara, six months old.
The children spoke only English,
but the parents, Henry and Elsie

could talk with me in Plautdietsch.
The house was big, two stories.
Louise took me upstairs
to show me which bedroom would be mine.
She was eager to show off her own room.
Confidently, this little girl said,
"Because you don't know English,
you can ask me to help with your homework."
I thought I would surely like living with this family,
but on the ride home, anxiety rose up in me.
One more week until school.
Tomorrow, the Pankratzes would come for me.

XLVII. Yet Again, A New School

My anxiety did not interfere too much with enjoying school.
Before even one month was up,
I realized I liked it!
I didn't mind being in class with seventh graders,
even though I was four years older than most students.
Jean and Roberta, who knew Plautdietsch,
were kind to me and they helped me
when understanding was challenging.
I got along well in the home economics class
because the teacher was so friendly.
I think she tried to build up my confidence.
"Look at how nice Justina made her stitches!"
she announced, holding up my potholder project.
I felt my face flush red.
Sewing a potholder seemed silly,
because I had already put together a wool suit—
with fully-lined jacket, shoulder pads.
and bound buttonholes.
Still, I found myself wishing I could be with my age group.
I watched them in the cafeteria,
and mostly, I felt that I was invisible to them.
Only one girl, a tall red-haired junior,
Elfrieda, smiled when she saw me pass.
(But, at least they put me with girls my age in Sunday School—
for only one hour, on Sunday morning,
hardly enough time to get to know anyone).

Justa's Escape

I remembered I once had friends—
Annie, Lenie, and Victor (and others).
back in Amsterdam.

XLVIII. Study, Study, and Study Some More

I finished grade seven that May,
but I knew I must keep on learning before fall.
The principal was pleased with my grades
and willing to let me accelerate
into grades eight and nine—
that is, if Uncle John tutored me all summer
in literature and American History.
I also needed to find a paying job—
one to send money and food to Mama and Anna.
Uncle John and Aunt Mary had paid for my trip to America
and so I wanted to pay them back their $258.00.
My goal was also to save money for nursing school.
I earned five dollars a week from the Pankratzes
for housework and babysitting Barbara.
Churches paid me five dollars to talk about my refugee life.
and even though it pained me to share,
I did it, if they asked.
Every cent went into the bank
for sending food packages to Mama.

Before the summer flew by
I heard that Uncle Ben would visit from Canada.
Uncle Ben was like a ghost to me;
Mama had spoken of him all the time,
but I'd never seen him with my own eyes.
Now I knew what having butterflies in your stomach meant.

I could not touch lunch before we left to meet Uncle Ben at the
bus station.
Finally, a bus pulled in.
A man, an older version of my brother Gerhard,
stepped down and walked directly to me.
"You are my sister's daughter.
I can see that," he said simply.
His eyes filled with tears
and mine misted over.
I nodded.
We looked at each other.
Uncle Ben seemed quiet.
I was shy.
After all, we were strangers.
He asked questions about each of my brothers,
He'd known all the Neufeld children,
except for us two youngest,
brother Ben and me.
Every time we mentioned Mama,
a shadow moved over Uncle Ben's face.
Should I tell him how much Mama talked of him,
how very much she wanted to see all her brothers again?
Somehow, it felt as if it was a secret
I needed to protect,
but maybe it was myself I was guarding.
Would letting it go mean I would open up this wound?
Embarrassed, would I shriek like a wild animal
if I talked about it?
Instead, I held it in until bedtime,
then cried in the private darkness before sleep.

Uncle Ben stayed just two days.
I admitted only to myself
that I was relieved to see him go.
Only then did the tight feeling in my chest leave me.
What should I report to Mama—

XLVIII. Study, Study, and Study Some More

that I was glad for Uncle Ben to go home?
That we both felt too much pain
when we talked about her?

XLIX. High School Graduation

One day the principal met me in the cafeteria.
"Justina, you will get your diploma this spring.
if your good grades continue."
"What does he mean?" asks my friend Elizabeth.
"You've been in high school only two years."
"I don't know what he means,
but you heard him," I reply.
To me, it means I can work full-time,
to earn money
to send food to Mama, I think.

Although now I usually sit with girls
closer to my age in the cafeteria,
I frequently join the girls I started with
in seventh grade.
I can never get used to students
not eating all the food on their plates
When I see them throw food into the garbage bucket,
I turn away. I pray,
"Father, forgive them they know not what they do,"
I graduate from high school—
only one year older than the other graduates.

L. Surprise! Surprises!

"Tell me about your dress
for the senior banquet,"
says Elizabeth.
"I am not going,"
I say piteously.
"No boy has asked me.
To those boys,
I don't even exist."
"Bah!"
Elizabeth scoffs,
"You don't need a boy—
You can be my date!"

But, two days later,
a boy follows me
from the school building.
When no one else is in sight,
he hurries to catch up with me.
"Would you be my date?
To the banquet I mean?"
I can hardly hear him.

I have seen him around,
but know nothing about him.
He reminds me of myself—
shy, uncomfortable,
awkward.

"Yes, I accept," I say,
maybe too quickly.
My dress is a hand-me-down—
it doesn't really fit.
I do not enjoy the banquet at all,
but I love the fact
that a boy has noticed me
and has given me a beautiful corsage.

Elizabeth and I
remain friends for life.
Even though,
I had a date,
and she didn't.
She gives me a hardcover book—
covered in maroon shades—
paisley cloth—
A whole book of empty pages.
"It is beautiful.
But what is it for?"
"The pages are for you to fill.
Before you forget,
promise to write your life story."
I nod.
I have kept my promise.

Afterword

Dear Reader,

You may wonder what happened to my family, and how I adjusted to my new home.

Shortly before my brother, his family, and I boarded the ship to come to America, we had made contact with my mother's brothers in Canada. One day we received a letter from Uncle Ben; our mother had survived the war. Mama, my sister, Anna, and Tante had been exiled from Poland to a Siberian Gulag, (a labor camp). The long journey in cattle cars, the cold, and lack of food took a toll on them. Tante had died of starvation shortly after they arrived there. Tante had been like a grandma to me, loving me unconditionally. My grief was almost unbearable. It was doubtful that Mama and Anna would survive much longer. My greatest wish was to see Mama again.

After we arrived in the US, we learned through the Red Cross and by networking with other refugees that two of my brothers, Dietrich and Willy, had also been exiled to Kazakhstan, a Russian Republic. Dietrich was able to secure our mother's and Anna's release from the Gulag to bring them to Kazakhstan, saving them from starvation. I corresponded with Mama until she died in 1965.

Over the first couple of years, I hoped to visit her, and Gerhard tried to facilitate her immigration to the United States. However, because of the invisible Iron Curtain, (strained political relations between the Soviet Union and the United States) that was not possible.

Two brothers, Jacob (and his family) and Ben immigrated to Canada. Papa and my brothers, Peter and Franz, were never found in spite of extensive searches through the Red Cross and other organizations. Brother Johann found Mama through miraculous circumstances and so we connected with him; he also lived in Kazakhstan, He was able to immigrate to Germany and I visited him numerous times.

After graduating from high school, I worked to earn money to continue my education. In 1955 I received my RN degree and in 1957 a BS degree in Nursing Administration. In 1983, while working in the field of mental health, I earned an MA degree in Gerontology.

One of my great fortunes in life was that I was married to a most loving man, Floyd Bartel. We were married for almost 22 years when he died. Floyd was an unexpected gift, a true soulmate.

I wrote my memoirs, *A Family Torn Apart,* published in 2004.

I am grateful to many people who helped me achieve my goals. I feel blessed to have worked in the healing profession, enabling me to heal myself.

Justina Neufeld

Acknowledgements

This book would not have been written without much help from others.

First, I owe gratitude to Leslie Wright, sixth grade teacher. After speaking to her class about being displaced during WWII, the students wrote thank-you letters to me, telling me what they had learned about that time in history. So Leslie encouraged me to write my memoirs for young adults.

Much gratitude goes to Beverley Buller. I asked Beverley, a middle school librarian, to recommend children's books for me to read. From the start she and I spent considerable time drinking coffee and talking about my writing. She was willing to coach me as I struggled to choose a format. Beverley provided me with a list of children's books and read my manuscript, one chapter at a time and gave helpful suggestions. She believed that children would relate to a true-life story on an emotional level, learn a bit of history and the effects of war.

I want to thank my very special writers' group, Loretta Baumgartner, Rachel Poling and Lois Preheim. The group met twice a month to read each other our writing. They listened attentively and gave valuable feedback.

A very special thank-you to my young critics whom I had selected early on to read a sample of the stories to test if they were age appropriate. Edel, age 13, was very generous with her red pen. Edel corrected spelling, changed sentence structure and gave advice and encouragement. Tessa and Claire, sisters, age 11, both gave positive feedback. Elizabeth age 12, wanted to read "more" chapters. These young peoples' responses encouraged me to continue with the project.

My heartfelt gratitude goes to Katherine Bartel, my dear step-daughter artist, who created the book cover.

I owe my deepest gratitude to my friend and editor, Russell Binkley, PhD. Rus spent many hours editing my draft in addition to teaching full time and taking annual trips to Kenya. I doubt this book would have been published without his dedication and persistence. Thank-you, Rus.

9 781666 795264